11 x 7 1

D0195374

# 20
# Questions
# to Ask
## Before Selling
## Your Home

James Edgar
and
Jean Jessop Hervey
Point Loma Branch Library

## Steve Holzner and
## Nancy Conner

CAREER
PRESS
THE CAREER PRESS, INC.
Franklin Lakes, NJ

**20 QUESTIONS TO ASK BEFORE SELLING YOUR HOME**

EDITED BY KATE HENCHES

Cover design by Lu Rossman/Digi Dog Design

Printed in the U.S.A. by Book-mart Press

To order this title, please call toll-free 1-800-CAREER-1 (NJ and Canada: 201-848-0310) to order using VISA or MasterCard, or for further information on books from Career Press.

The Career Press, Inc., 3 Tice Road, PO Box 687,
Franklin Lakes, NJ 07417
**www.careerpress.com**

**Library of Congress Cataloging-in-Publication Data**

Holzner, Steve, 1957-

20 questions to ask before selling your home / by Steve Holzner and Nancy Conner.

p. cm. — (20 questions to ask)

ISBN 1-5614-821-1 (paper)

1. House selling—United States. 2. Residential real estate—United States. I. Title: Twenty questions to ask before selling your home. II. Title: Questions to ask before selling your home. III. Conner, Nancy, 1961- IV. Title. V. Series.

HD259.H65 2005

643'.12--dc22

2005042171

# Contents

# Introduction

Most likely, your home is your biggest investment. So making the decision to sell your house is a big step that requires careful thought and planning. Are you ready to sell—both emotionally and in terms of the property's condition? When is the best time to put a house on the market? Should you use a real estate agent? What happens if you get an offer—or if you *don't* get an offer? What are the legal requirements?

Selling a house is a complex process, and, because your investment in your house is probably a large one, you stand to gain—or lose thousands of dollars as you proceed. To get the best return on your investment you want to do things *right*.

As a homeowner, you've probably been through the other side of the equation. When you bought your home, you may have worked with a Realtor, learned about home inspections, gone through the escrow process, and signed a mountain of papers at the closing. Things look different from the seller's point of view. You'll still have to decide whether you want to work with a Realtor, but you need to start thinking about the sale long before the first potential buyer walks through the door: deciding on the best asking price, when to list your house, how to deal with structural problems, how to increase "curb appeal" and prepare the interior for showings, and how to find buyers through advertising and open houses. When an offer comes in, you need to evaluate it from the seller's point of view, understand the legal jargon of a purchase agreement, and know how to negotiate. And the seller has responsibilities up to, at, and even after closing that you may not have considered.

This book answers the questions most sellers ask about how to sell a house—and even some you probably haven't considered. From preparing your house (and yourself) for a sale, through offers and negotiations, to what happens at closing and after, you'll find the answers you need to sell your house right, avoid potential pitfalls, and get the best return on your investment.

# $Q$uestion 1

## Is This the Right Move?

So you're thinking about taking the plunge? Congratulations! Selling a house can be a terrific experience: one that sweetens your life—and your bank account. But selling a house is also a big step, and there are few people available to tell you, with total certainty, whether or not this is the right step for you. It would be great if there were some expert who could tell you just how happy you'd be with the deal one, two, or 10 years down the line, but such experts are in short supply.

Is this the right time to sell? Will you regret the deal?

How can you know, exactly?

Selling a house is a big step, and one that sometimes has unexpected emotional and financial consequences. This chapter starts the whole process by looking at this major transaction in overview.

Sometimes, whether or not you should sell isn't a question. Your job has been relocated, and you've decided to go with it; you want to be closer to relatives; you've retired and decided to sell the house, now that it's just the two of you; or circumstances have changed and those big mortgage payments no longer look so manageable. In any of these cases, your choice has already been made: feel free to turn to the next chapter.

But more frequently, you have to make your own decision. And you can't know, exactly, how things are going to turn out. You can, however, do enough work beforehand to know whether or not you're comfortable with the deal, even if you're feeling nervous right now. And that's what this chapter is about: how to know, as far as possible, if this is the right move for you.

# Keep a Cool Head

The single most important thing in real estate is to keep a cool head so that you can see your way clearly. This may not sound so important if this is your first real estate deal, but people who've made many deals will tell you it's vital to stay calm. When someone ends up in a bad deal, it's almost always for one of two reasons: he either got too emotionally committed, or didn't do enough work checking the property and the paperwork.

> *The single most important thing in real estate is to keep a cool head so that you can see your way clearly.*

Selling is a waiting game, and that's tough on the nerves. Real estate deals stretch out over months of looking, viewing, bidding, and anticipating, and each day adds a little more push to the process until, before you know it, things have snowballed emotionally. And, suddenly, *you just have to have make that deal*, no matter what the cost or the trouble.

To aggravate the situation, there's often a huge emotional cost to selling a house: after all, it's *your home*. Are you prepared to move out and let strangers move in? To never see the inside of the current home again? To let them paint it in that ridiculous orange? Do you know where you're going, and feel sure it's the right choice? All of those are items of which you need to be as sure as you can be.

These are reasons you must be sure to have a clear head at all times, and stay a little detached from the deal. Sit down and *take the time* to make sure you're clear mentally and emotionally about the process. It sounds obvious, but we've seen many, many deals end up on the rocks because people didn't really watch where they were going. When you've got a clear overview of what's going on, you'll be able to see your way clearly.

> *Selling a house usually takes months and it's not a decision to take lightly.*

# Work Through the Process Mentally

There are many stages coming up in this process: the decision to sell, listing your house, showing it, making a deal, working with (possibly neurotic) buyers, handling the legal issues, living through the closing, moving, paying taxes—and much more, as you can see by glancing through this book. Selling a house usually takes months, and it's not a decision to take lightly. So work through the process mentally. Are you ready to sell your home?

You also need to prepare yourself for what's ahead. You're going to have to come up with a price, and then try to stick to it (see Question 6). You're going to have to be wary of questionable buyers. You should know, for example, that many buyers will keep adding more and more conditions on the sale as time passes. Watch out for vague clauses in purchase contracts offered to you by buyers that allows them to keep piling on more and more items (such as repainting the trim, adding new gutters, or performing expensive landscaping) over the months that the deal takes. Some buyers will do that on purpose, making the deal seem sweet initially, and then requiring more and more after the seller has agreed and feels committed. You are, of course, also going to have to deal with moving out and leaving your house behind.

## When You're Clear About the Process, You'll Know What to Do

There are a lot of emotions and money involved, and now's not the time to make a decision you'll regret for years to come. Focus on staying somewhat detached in order to see your way clearly. When working to make your decisions consciously, you'll know if selling is right for you. Otherwise, things are going to feel murky, and there's no way you can really know if you're doing the right thing. *Always* stay in control of what's going on.

Be sure selling is the right move for you; then, start with a cool head, and make sure you get all the facts. In the end, only you can decide if the deal is the right one for you. But when you're operating consciously and you have the facts laid out in front of you, things will fall into place.

Always stay in control of what you're doing in real estate, and the deal will treat you right.

Okay, on to the selling process. Turn to Question 2.

# $Q$uestion 2

## Is This the Right Time to Sell?

Should you sell? Should you hold on for a while longer? There are two things to do to get as clear an answer as you can: know the market, and know the consequences.

## Know the Market

If you have the luxury of deciding to sell now or later, it's worth taking time to get to know how the market is doing, especially when it comes to house prices in your neighborhood. Are prices going up or down? Are they near a peak or a trough? What's going to happen in the future?

Is this right time to sell?

If you're looking for the right price, and can wait for it, you should watch the market and its trend (up or down). If you've been in a hot market and house sales are starting to slow, you're probably near the *peak*. If nothing is moving at all unless it's significantly underpriced, you're in a *trough*. If prices are on the upswing, it might be worth waiting; if they're starting to slide, it may be a good time to sell.

If you've been thinking about selling, you've probably considered this issue. You may have a rough idea of what the market has been doing, but you can sharpen your take on that in several ways.

> *If prices are on the upswing, it might be worth waiting;*
> *if they're starting to slide, it may be a good time to sell.*

To know the market, do your research. Local newspapers often have house sales data for the last year or two. And it's all the better if the newspaper is searchable online. If this information is not available to you, look for the house ads in the paper and watch the prices. There might be a weekly real estate supplement. Dive in and get all the data out of it you can. Do you want to know if the market is going up or down in an area? Watch how long it takes to sell individual houses in that supplement. This will give you a handle on how things are going in the short term. For a longer-term picture, you've got to do more research, as discussed in this section.

Newspapers also usually track real estate trends over time, so keep watching them for more data. If you can't find what you want, give the paper a call and see if someone can help you find articles discussing local real estate trends.

There are many professionals out there whose business it is to know the market, and scoping them out can give you plenty of targeted insight. The foremost among them are Realtors, of course. Whether or not you're going to use a Realtor (see the next chapter), you can get a good feel for the market and whether it's worth waiting just by talking with one of them. As we're going to discuss in Question 4, you can get Realtors to come to your house and discuss the sale with you, including what the market is doing. (But be careful; Realtors make their livings by making house deals happen, so it's to their advantage to convince you that now's a good time to sell.)

Many realty offices do keep track of what the market's been doing, so you can also ask to see any data they've been collecting. Be upfront and call several offices regarding this— if you decide to use a Realtor, the more you know about him or her, the better.

Other people to talk to are tax assessors (call your county's assessment office), whose business it is to know whether house prices are going up or down, and house appraisers. House appraisers (see "Appraisers" or "Real Estate Appraisers" in the phone book) are professionals whose job it is to determine house values for banks, which they'll do for the buyer's lending institution in your house sale (we're going to talk more about appraisers in Question 5). Often, they'll talk about what the market has been doing in your area if you just give them a call and discuss it. We've been able to determine market conditions in several unfamiliar areas this way.

> *House appraisers are professionals whose job it is to determine house values for banks, which they'll do for the buyer's lending institution in your house sale.*

Researching online can help, especially if your county clerk's office lists sales data online. Some Websites, such as *www.terraxsite.com/wsj/index.cfm?page=residential*, can give you pricing data by area using interactive maps. Others, such as *www.wellsfargo.com/homesalesreport*, can list sales data in your area for houses during the last two years. (Note that URLs such as these can and do change frequently, and might not be the same by the time you read this.)

Get as much information as you can. To know the market in a specific area, get in tune with what's going on there. Watch those "For Sale" and "Open House" signs. We've seen neighborhoods where there were few houses for sale until something triggered a change (the prime rate went up, for example, which means mortgage rates eventually go up, which means buyers will start to hesitate). Almost overnight, those areas were peppered with "For Sale" signs. If you see something like that happening, you're pretty near the peak (and note that a glut of houses for sale can start to bring prices down).

Another thing to keep in mind when deciding whether this is the right time to sell your house is that selling houses is a seasonal process, with most being sold in the spring and summer (often so that moves can be done before the kids have to go to the new school), tapering off in the fall and winter. November and December are traditionally the slowest months. (More on this in Question 7.)

# Know the Consequences

Another part of deciding whether it's time to sell your house is keeping in mind the consequences of that sale. This one's not so easy to sum up. There's a lot to think about, which means that we'll be discussing such consequences throughout the book. But here's an overview of some of the things you should start taking into consideration:

➲ Are you likely to lose money in the sale?

➲ Are there any prepayment penalties if you pay off your mortgage early?

➲ Is the deed in good order, without *liens* or *encumbrances*?

➲ Are you prepared to pay for the survey the buyer's lender will require?

➲ Will you have to pay back some or all of the deductions you took for depreciation?

➲ Can you pay the capital gains taxes, which can be hefty—or do you qualify for an exemption? (More on this in Question 18.)

➲ Are you willing to pay Realtor commissions (typically 4 to 6 percent of the sale price)?

➲ How much will moving costs be?

➲ How much will the closing costs and fees be (see Question 16)?

➲ Are you liable for any other taxes or costs?

As you'll see in Question 7, preparing a house for sale can be a lot of work. Some relatively cosmetic touches can have a big effect on house prices, as we'll discuss. A new coat of paint can help tremendously, as can other relatively inexpensive items such as shutters (made of plastic these days, and easy to attach), lawn care, and other items. Some people estimate that a single tree can add 5 to 7 percent to the selling price of a house—not a bad investment. But the work might all add up to more than you want to do.

So, is this the right time to sell? When you know the trend in the market: if it's going up, it might be smart to wait; if it's going down, it might be smart to sell. And you know the consequences of selling, you know the answer. This chapter got the ball rolling on those topics, but they're both big issues and more on them is coming right up.

# Question 3

## Should I Sell the House Myself?

An estimated 20 percent of all residential house sales are "For Sale By Owner" (FSBO, popularly pronounced "fizz bo") sales, where the owners sell their own house. Selling your house yourself offers significant advantages, but there are also many pitfalls. This chapter takes a look at both.

## The Attractions

For most people, the major attraction is that you can save a good portion of the 5 to 6 percent commission of the selling price that Realtors will charge (the seller pays this commission). You might also want to keep control of the process, because when a Realtor is involved, all communication goes through the Realtor, which can introduce its own set of complications. Selling a house yourself usually works best under a certain set of circumstances:

- ➲ You may have a buyer already, in which case much of what a Realtor does—finding a buyer—isn't necessary.

- ➲ You may be familiar with the process and just need a lawyer. If you're a pro at this already, then you may feel comfortable going FSBO.

- ➲ You may know the neighborhood and the prices well, and feel that you can handle the whole process.

- ➲ You may feel you'd be more motivated than a real estate agent to sell your house.

- ➲ Your house may sell itself. If you're in a hot real estate market, buyers may just be waiting to snap your house up.

Keep in mind that unless you've already got a deal, you'll have to get the word out there, which can mean signs and advertising. (Houses are even being sold on eBay these days. If you list there, you can purchase an inexpensive house-selling kit, complete with "For Sale" signs. But that can entail all the problems of selling long-distance to people who might not have even seen the house.)

# The Dangers

Besides the chance to take control of the process and potentially save a lot of money, there are significant risks involved in selling your house yourself. The foremost among these is the possibility of legal problems—there are many out there waiting to trap you.

The usual real estate sales team is made up of a Realtor, a lawyer, and a number of other possible team members: an escrow officer (to handle money transactions between you and the seller, although lawyers can also often do this), a tax advisor, and a housing appraiser and/or inspector. Although a real estate lawyer can handle most of the legal issues you might come across, from checking the buyer's purchase agreement contract to filing forms with the county and state on the sale, the real estate lawyer can't necessarily handle it all.

For example, as a Realtor can tell you, you have to avoid discriminating against buyers on the basis of race, color, religion, sex, handicap, familial status, or national origin. Your state may have additional requirements, such as not discriminating on the basis of sexual preference. Check the Office of Fair Housing and Equal Opportunity (*www.hud.gov*) for pamphlets and information, and read the rest of this book for other legal issues you might come up against. For example, if you fail to disclose everything your state and federal governments require, such as the presence of lead paint in the house, you leave yourself wide open to termination of the sales agreement or even a lawsuit. There are other, non-legal issues that a Realtor can help with as well, such as knowing how to prepare your house for sale and how to qualify buyers to avoid deadbeats.

*Check the Office of Fair Housing and Equal Opportunity (www.hud.gov) for pamphlets and information on laws against discrimination.*

Just like any other product for sale, your house won't find buyers unless it's advertised. FSBO homeowners must pay their own advertising costs—and the *only* way to get your home listed in the multiple listing service (MLS) is to go through a Realtor. (There are, however, some discount brokers who will list your home on the MLS for a flat fee of several hundred dollars. Do a Web search for *"MLS"* and *"flat fee"* to comparison shop.) The MLS, described in Question 4, is the primary sales tool for getting potential buyers into your home.

If you go FSBO, you also run the risk of not getting a good price; buyers often think FSBO means "cheap" because they hope to take advantage of inexperienced sellers (and they also know you're not paying a real estate commission). And Realtors are usually skilled negotiators when it comes to price. (Although technically Realtors aren't supposed to do more than communicate your requirements when it comes to price, they can sometimes advise you in some depth.)

You're also going to be using up a lot of your time. There may be things you have to do that you've never done before, such as getting a title report, opening an escrow, having a survey done, getting a payoff demand for your mortgage, and so on. A real estate lawyer will be able to tell you about these things, and usually can do them for you as well.

The purchase agreement you sign with the buyer is legally binding, and although a Realtor can give you professional advice about such contracts, it's best to take such agreements to lawyers. Purchase agreements may have many contingencies in them, such as repairs the buyer wants done, and you have to know how to deal with such contingencies.

If you do want to go FSBO, it's a good idea to qualify buyers by asking that they're preapproved by a lender—they should have a letter to show you, or let you call a lending officer. You can also get the buyer's permission to ask the lender about the likelihood of approval, or even do a credit check if you want (your bank can often help you with the process).

All in all, there's a lot to do yourself if you're going FSBO,

> *The purchase agreement you sign with the buyer is legally binding...it's best to take such agreements to lawyers.*

as detailed in this and the coming chapters. Realtors have told us that 90 percent of FSBO sales end up going with Realtors, but that seems like too high an estimate. Be prepared for one thing: Realtors will call FSBOs to see if you want to list with them. Be be prepared to field some over-the-phone pitches.

Another thing to keep in mind is that, if you're going FSBO, it's a good idea to say, "Will cooperate with buyer's agents" in your ads, which means you might pay a half commission (2 to 3 percent) to agents acting as buyer's agents for potential buyers. If you don't want Realtors involved at all, your ad should state, "Principals only." That means you'll only deal with the actual person who wants to buy your house.

Also bear in mind that it's free to get a Realtor's point of view. You can have Realtors come to your house and give you presentations on why they're the best one to sell your house (as we'll discuss in Question 4). You can get a lot of good advice this way, get many questions answered—even on some legal issues—and ultimately decide whether going with a Realtor is right for you.

# How Much Will I Save?

You're probably not going to save as much as you might think—not the full 5 to 6 percent commission of the selling price an agent would charge. For one thing, there are usually advertising costs to think about. These can be considerable, especially if you plan to advertise in the paper's real estate supplement.

If your buyer has a Realtor acting as a buyer's agent, you might have to pay that agent a half commission as well.

Bear in mind that most buyers will expect you to lower the price if you're selling your house FSBO. That's not to say that you have to, but that's often the expectation.

If you do decide to go FSBO, we really recommend that you get a good lawyer. There are potential legal snags throughout the entire process, from signing the buyer's purchase agreement, which is a legally binding contract, to filing papers with the recorder of deeds, and more. See the section "Getting a Good Lawyer" in Question 10 for more details.

# Question 4

## Should I Get a Realtor?

Question 3 discussed selling your house For Sale By Owner, or FSBO. In nearly every case, though, we're going to recommend that you get a Realtor to help handle the sale. Although we don't practice as Realtors, both of us have taken the required training classes for Realtors in New York State and passed the state certification exams. We know that these days, things are so complex when you sell a house that the chances are good that you might run afoul of some rule you didn't even know about—everything from not understanding the full disclosure laws about the condition of your house to being accused of discriminatory selling practices.

# What Does a Realtor Do for You?

It's the Realtor's job to sell your house; if they don't, they don't get paid. There's a lot they'll do for you. Here are some of the salient items:

- ➲ Walk you through the whole process from beginning to end. They've usually been through it many times.

- ➲ Help you set a reasonable selling price for the house, based on what they think will sell. (Be a little careful here, though. Because it's in the Realtor's interest to sell the house, some Realtors might set the selling price a little low.)

- ➲ Provide comps in the neighborhood, giving you an idea of what's selling and for how much.

- ➲ Advertise your property, both on the big listing service—the Multiple Listing Service (MLS) available to any Realtor and on *Realtor.com*— and in local sources such as newspapers and real estate supplements.

- ➲ Show your house to potential buyers.

- ➲ Qualify potential buyers so you don't waste your time.

- ➲ Negotiate sales contracts and alert you to risks (as will your lawyer).

- ➲ Keep you abreast of laws, such as full disclosure requirements.

- ➲ Give you an estimate of your closing costs.

- ➲ Be present at closing (along with your lawyer) to review documents and help answer questions.

# How Do I Choose a Realtor?

The terms *Realtor*, *broker*, and *agent* are sometimes used interchangeably, but they're not the same. A Realtor, someone licensed to represent buyers and sellers in property transactions in a given state, can be either a broker or an agent. A broker is one who is licensed to handle real estate transactions, and an agent (sometimes called a licensed salesperson) works for a broker. You need to be a broker to run a real estate agency; usually half of an agent's commission goes to the broker. Sometimes agents take the broker exams but don't elect to start their own agencies; instead, they keep working for a broker and are known as *associate brokers*. There are also discount brokers available who will charge you smaller commissions for reduced services—before agreeing to work with one, make sure you know, upfront, what a discount broker will and won't do.

> *If you do it right, you'll take some time to pick the right Realtor. You can have Realtors come to your home and give you a presentation on why they'd be the best one to sell your house. Such presentations typically take 20 to 40 minutes, and are designed to sell you on the Realtor who makes the presentation. Take your time, listen, and get several Realtors to come over.*

Ask whether the Realtor will advise you on how to prepare your home for the market, whether he or she will show you comps in the area and help you set a price. Ask the Realtor about his or her track record—what he or she has sold in the area, the dates of those sales, what commission you'll be charged, and whether or not he or she is a member of the Multiple Listing Service. You can also ask if he or she has any special training, such as GRI (Graduate, Realtor Institute) or CRS (Certified Residential Specialist) designations, and, if so, just what those designations mean.

Does the Realtor show enthusiasm for the deal and for your house? Has she or he done any research before talking to you? Do you like the looks of his or her ads in the local newspaper's real estate supplement? Is he or she accessible, both during, and, if need be, after hours? Do you get along well? Ask for references and talk to sellers with whom she or he has worked in the past.

One of the most common ways that people choose a Realtor is to ask friends for recommendations. Realtors know that very well, and often go to great lengths to expand their pools of friends and satisfied clients.

# What Do You Sign?

You sign a listing agreement (also called a *listing contract*) between you and the licensed real estate broker, authorizing the broker (and the agents) to find someone to purchase your house. *Don't* do a verbal agreement—always get it in writing. Here are the standard forms of this agreement (go over any such agreement with a lawyer before signing):

- ➲ **Exclusive right to agency:** The broker's agency is the only agency that can sell your house. This still allows you to sell your house yourself, so brokers aren't very fond of this type.

- ➲ **Exclusive right to sell:** The broker's agency is the only one allowed to sell your house. You can't sell it yourself without paying the commission.

➲ **Open listing:** A non-exclusive authorization to sell your house, along with other agencies, and you can also sell it. You'll have to pay a commission to the first broker who produces a ready, willing, and able buyer. Beware, though, that open-listing houses often can't be listed on the MLS.

The most common is the exclusive right to sell; some brokers won't sign other types of listing agreements because they could end up competing with you as a seller. If you sign an exclusive right to sell agreement, make sure it has a termination date so you're not stuck in it forever; you can even ask for a termination clause that you can invoke if you want to get out of it.

*Don't let an agency sit on your listing without advertising it for a while—it could be waiting to see if someone inside the agency can sell it, which means they'd collect both seller's and buyer's agent commissions. Tell them to advertise your house immediately.*

Note especially that if you sign a listing agreement and the Realtor brings you a "ready, willing, and able" buyer at the price you're asking for and you don't sell, you could end up owing some Realtor fees.

## How Much Will It Cost?

Typically, if you use a Realtor, it's going to cost you 5 percent to 6 percent of the selling price in commissions. (Bear in mind that that money will come from the money you get for the sale minus the money you still have to pay off on your mortgage.) Overall, if you use a Realtor, it'll typically cost you 7 to 10 percent of the selling price to sell your house if you include all fees (this estimate excludes capital gains taxes).

Feel queasy about spending all that money? Take a look at the previous question on selling your house yourself. However, we recommend, while saving money on the process where you can, you use a Realtor.

## Some Drawbacks to Using a Realtor

There are some potential drawbacks to using a Realtor of which you should be aware. You may feel that a Realtor is not giving you and your sale enough attention or enough exposure. That can be a serious problem; if it persists, get a new Realtor. Realtors can also sometimes be inaccessible (..although not to the extent lawyers are). If you can't get in touch with your Realtor, that's not a good sign. Potential buyers might be having the same trouble.

Here's another potential problem: Realtors are human, and sometimes they can end up stifling communication between buyer and seller (such communication is always supposed to go through the Realtor). This is rare, but once or twice, we've felt it necessary to circumvent a Realtor and speak directly with the other party in order to save the deal. As mentioned, this kind of thing is rare, and Realtors frown on it very much, but it can happen.

# $Q$uestion 5

## How Do I Know What My House Is Really Worth?

Congratulations! You've decided to sell. Your first order of business is to get an idea what your house is really worth today, in market terms. Even if you think you know the answer, you should check on it. The market is changing very fast these days, and it can really pay to be up to date.

Determining what's called the *fair market value* (FMV) of your house is a bit of an art, and we'll discuss it in this chapter. One thing you need to bear in mind: FMV is the fair *market* value; the emphasis is not so much on the *fair* part. The value of your house in people's eyes is what others are willing to pay for it in the current market, not necessarily the value you think it should sell for. And that idea can take a lot of getting used to.

Note that FMV is what you should be able to get for your house, but it may not be the price at which you want to list your house; as you will read in Question 6, you may want to ask for more in order to end up getting what you want. The amount you add to the FMV is up to you, of course, and it depends on how hot the market is and how hot (or cool) it is likely to become. In a seller's market, markup may be 25 percent or even more.

## Ask a Realtor for an FMV Estimate

You might think of Realtors as specialists in setting asking prices, but they're experts on what houses actually sell for as well. The prices you see in the paper are the asking prices, but keep in mind that the prices houses actually sell at are going to be different. Selling prices used to be listed in the paper too, and they may be listed in yours, but that's going out of style these days.

> *When we're not familiar with an area we ask our Realtor friends who are familiar. They're able to tell us what houses are selling for in that region.*

Getting an FMV estimate from a Realtor is different from asking a Realtor to set an asking price. As discussed in Question 5, setting asking prices is what they do for a living. Giving you an FMV estimate is usually a more informal process.

Over the years, we've become friends with many Realtors in many different areas. When we're not familiar with an area, we ask our Realtor friends who are familiar. They're usually able to tell us what houses are selling for in that region. And they can take a look at a house and give us a pretty accurate estimate of what it would sell for.

That's what you should do here: talk to a Realtor and ask him or her what he or she thinks your house could sell for. Make it clear that you're not asking him or her to list the house, you're just starting to think about it and would like his or her estimate of how much you could actually get for your house. Most Realtors would be glad to help out, because they know their help might ultimately result in a listing. And if you find a Realtor who's just too busy to help you, that's also advance warning that you might not want to list with that person.

It's easy enough to check this out. Just make an appointment with a Realtor, or call and ask him or her what's involved in finding out what you might be able to sell your house for. This is a very common first step in selling any house, and Realtors are used to getting these kinds of questions. In fact, many realty offices keep track of selling prices by region, so finding your house's FMV may turn out to be a snap. And from there, you can turn to Question 6 to set the price at which you want to list your house.

## Ask an Appraiser

Another way to determine the FMV of a house is to use an *appraiser*, whose business it is to determine exactly what the FMV is. You should be able to find them listed under "Appraisers" or "Real Estate Appraisers" in the phone book. This way of determining how much your house is worth will cost several hundred dollars, but you'll get an accurate idea because the lending institutions that give mortgages to the buyers who will buy your house use appraisers to determine a house's FMV.

The appraiser may ask you about the value of recent comparable house sales in the area; if you happen to have the answers, tell them. If not, the appraiser will check into it for you; because you're paying for the appraisal, the appraiser should do any needed legwork on that.

## Check Your Assessment

In earlier days, a house's tax assessment (not appraisal) might have little to do with its FMV because the assessment might have been done many years ago and never updated. Or it might have been done at a fraction, typically 50 percent or 80 percent, of FMV. But these days, more and more municipalities are assessing every year or two, and at 100 percent market value, because they want to squeeze more taxes out of property owners.

If your tax assessment is up to date and you know what fraction of FMV it's intended to represent, it's often a good ballpark figure for a selling price. Tax assessors are familiar with literally all the houses in your area, so they have access to housing sales data and comps (comparable properties). If your assessment is significantly off from what you think it should be, don't trust it, but it can otherwise be a good guide. In many communities, you can ask for periodic reassessments.

## Check Your Neighborhood

Many homeowners already have a fairly good idea of what their house is worth, particularly if they're contemplating selling, because they've kept in touch. One way of keeping in touch is to watch house sales in your area.

Keep in mind that the asking price of a house is most often not the same as its selling price. Don't be misled into tracking merely the asking prices for houses in your area if you want to determine how much you can actually get for your house; make sure you get the selling prices. (On the other hand, if you want to determine a good listing price for your house, watching your neighborhood is a good idea.)

So a good source of information is to ask your neighbors. House worth is a topic most homeowners like to discuss in depth these days.

## Take Condition Into Consideration

Once you've looked at the assessed value of your house, think about any recent renovations or repairs you've done. How much have you invested in improving your home since its last assessment? The dollar amount you've paid to improve your property may or may not correspond to the precise value added to the house, but it can provide a good ballpark figure. Sometimes, small changes to increase curb appeal will add much more in value than you spent to make those changes. Other times, a buyer might be pleased to know that the roof was replaced a year ago but might not think of that in terms of dollar value.

On the other hand, if your home is in need of significant repairs, this could lower its value beneath the current tax assessment. You're legally obliged to disclose any known problems, and buyers are likely to want the problem fixed or the price lowered as a condition of the sale. Either way, it'll cost you.

## Check Your Newspaper

As mentioned earlier in this chapter, newspapers used to list selling prices of houses. That tradition has been falling out of favor, but your newspaper may still carry that kind of information. If so, the staff at the paper should be able to tell you how to do research on recent sales in your area.

Even if your paper doesn't list housing selling prices, it might be able to help you determine your house's FMV. For example, we once bought a house for very close to the amount as the median house value for the area, as given by the local newspaper. Through the years, it was easy to track the house's FMV. All we had to do was to watch how the area's median house value changed, as listed in the paper.

Even if your house is not at the median house value, say, it's 10 percent off, you can still track how your house's FMV is changing by watching what happens to the median house value and then correcting for that 10 percent difference.

# $Q$uestion 6

## What Price Should I Ask?

This can be a tough question. If you pick a price that's too high, the market will let you know as your house sits there, unsold, for months. But what if you pick a price that's too low? You could lose a lot of money.

This chapter is all about determining an initial price for the house you're selling. But in the final analysis, it's what the market will bear that determines selling price. After you set your initial price, keep watching the market's response, as discussed at the end of this chapter, and adjust as needed. Unless you're just testing the market, the idea is to sell your house, after all.

We've known people who blindly say you should set a price just by adding 10 percent to your house's current worth, but using the same formula in all kinds of markets—buyer's, seller's, and in between—simply isn't going to work. You have to gauge the kind of market with which you're dealing and come up with a price to match. And one way of doing that is to work with professionals whose business it is to know that market: Realtors.

# Ask a Realtor

Realtors make their living by pricing house deals as accurately as they can (that's not to say they're all experts!). If you've decided to go with a Realtor, ask him or her what price you think you should set. The Realtor should present you with a Comparable Market Analysis (CMA) that will indicate for what comparable properties (comps) in your area, if available, have recently sold. Based on the FMV and a good knowledge of the market, your Realtor should be able to give you a good estimate on the listing price.

> *Note that the price suggested may not be what you want to hear. If so, be sure to ask you Realtor for details.*

However, we've heard stories where individual Realtors were far off the mark here, so get multiple price quotes, as part of the process of reviewing Realtors. If estimated listing prices cluster around a certain range, you can ignore the ones that are way off.

Note that the price suggested may not be what you want to hear. If so, be sure to ask your Realtor for the details. You don't have to accept his or her price, of course, and you can suggest raising it. But if you set it too high, the Realtor, whose income depends on making deals, may back off.

There are two things to be a little careful about here. Precisely because the agent's commission depends on selling your house, an agent may be more conservative on price than you'd like. He or she wants the house to move, and move fast. Some agents even set prices low for quick sales, so if you think the price is off, speak up.

On the other hand, some Realtors may talk up your house and its price in order to get your listing, a process called *buying a listing*. That doesn't mean your house will sell at the suggested price. What it does mean is that the agent will be able to impress his or her broker with the number of listings they're bringing in.

Also bear in mind that other Realtors will search by price using computers these days, so if you end up setting a price of $201,000, and buyers ask for a list of all houses priced at $200,000 or less, they'll never see yours. That's the reason many houses end up at prices such as $149,900, $259,000, and so on.

# Do Your Research

Another way to determine a good listing price is to do your own research. If you've got the time, watch the listing prices of other, comparable houses in the paper's housing supplement, if there is one. The selling picture will quickly come into focus if you do this.

> *The www.Realtor.com site is a good one because you can plug in you area, type of house, number of bedrooms, and so on in order to get as many matches as possible.*

Another way to do your research is online, either at your local newspaper's Website if it lets you track sales data, or at *www.Realtor.com*.

The *www.Realtor.com* site in particular is a good one, because you can plug in your area, type of house, number of bedrooms, and so on in order to get as many matches as possible. And you can do this kind of research at home or at your local library, using a Web browser.

As you use *www.Realtor.com* (and other sites like it), you'll become more familiar with the asking prices of houses like yours.

# Setting the Price

In the end, the price you set should be comparable to the asking prices of other houses similar to yours. If the price is greater than 10 percent more than the listing price of comparable houses, you may have trouble. Buyers comparison shop, and they usually have Realtors to advise them as well. Unless you're willing to wait for a long time or need a super-quick sale, we recommend that you stay within 10 percent of the asking prices of houses comparable to yours in the same area.

# Adjust as Needed

After you've set the price, you might have to adjust it over time. This varies from market to market, of course, but the fact that you can adjust your price as time goes on means that you don't have much to lose if you start a little high, especially in a market that's headed upward.

On the other hand, if your house sits on the market for an appreciable length of time, it's time to consider adjusting the price. Like it or not, selling a house is all about what the market will bear, and if it's not going to bear what you're asking, you have to either adjust for that fact or decide you'll try again at some later date.

# Question 7

## How Do I Prepare the House for Sale?

A big part of the process of selling is to prepare your house for sale. You're selling your house, and you want it to look as good as possible. An interesting thing happens with the vocabulary used to refer to your home here: Realtors will call it *selling a house*, while at the same time they talk to the buyers about *buying your home*.

It's sometimes not an easy thing to do, but now is when you must stop thinking about your home as your home, and start thinking about it as a house. The reason for this is that people have blind spots about their homes that they tolerate all the time, but that they would find problematic if they were buying a house.

That hinge that has to be treated in just the right way, that grubbiness around the kids' doorknob, the trim that got knocked off when you moved the refrigerator, those loose cabinet handles—you may be used to them, but potential buyers will not be. Cosmetic touches can count for a lot more than you might think.

# Preparing Your House

If you're like most house sellers, it's going to take a few weeks to prepare your house for sale, and you should allow for that much time. One of the best ways of preparing your house physically for sale is to ask an experienced Realtor about it. He can walk you through the process, and go through what's needed as he tours through your house.

Don't take offense at what they tell you. Sometimes, Realtors annoy people by treating their homes as wares to sell. But remember: that's the Realtor's business. If she's experienced, the advice she'll give you can be worth its weight in gold.

# All About Curb Appeal

The first thing that strikes potential buyers about your house is its appearance from the outside, whether they're getting out of their Realtor's car in front of your house or viewing MLS listings. That first impression is called *curb appeal*, and it's vitally important.

Realtors will be able to go through the specifics here, but here are some things to consider:

➲ Get rid of any external clutter. This is a big one: even a little clutter in your yard can, believe it or not, sabotage entire sales.

➲ External plantings can also play a big part. As mentioned in Question 2, some people estimate that a single tree can add 5 to 7 percent to the selling price of a house: not a bad investment. A flower garden, should you be so inclined, is also great.

➲ The lawn should be neatly trimmed and in good shape.

➲ The sidewalk, welcome mats (if any), steps, and so on—the whole approach to the house—should be clean and also in good shape.

➲ Painting is also very important and one of the quick-est things you can do to substantially improve selling price. We know that investors who buy houses and then sell them immediately (called house "flipping") nearly always put on a new coat of paint. Make sure the paint is in good repair, or consider retouching or painting. This is a big one.

➲ Windows are another favorite of house flippers. New windows can add many times their value to the sell-ing price of a house. Of course, it's a rare house seller who puts in all new windows, but make sure your windows are clean and look like they're in good condition.

Beware, however, of investing too much money in your house to sell it, and inadvertently pricing it out of the market in your area.

## The Smell of Freshly Baked Bread

Now to the inside of your house. We know one Realtor who advises sellers to make sure the kitchen has the smell of freshly baked bread for showings to make the house seem "homey." That may sound goofy, but you'll often read the ad-vice good smells in the kitchen— a roast, bread, cakes, and so on—make the house inviting.

It goes without saying that you're going to have to clean and scrub thoroughly, or hire someone to do it. The things your family may have gotten used to and no longer see will definitely be seen by potential buyers. For showings, all beds should be made, all clutter gone or hidden.

Add a bowl of fruit or a vase of flowers in the dining room, put out fresh towels in the bathroom—anything to give your house the feeling of invitation, of comfort, is a good idea. If you've got a fireplace, it's a great selling point and you should accent it by having lights near it, cleaning fireplace tools, and so on.

# Depersonalize

As hard as it seems, you should also consider removing personal materials, such as family photos or similar mementos, from display. We've seen showings where the whole family tree was on display in framed photos, or crocheted "Home Sweet Home" messages covered the furniture.

Don't do this. This kind of display makes buyers feel that they're intruding in your home—which they are, technically—and the more they feel it, the shorter the showing will be. The idea is to make *them* feel at home. So depersonalize things a little, if needed.

> *Consider removing personal materials, such as family photos or similar momentos from display. This kind of display makes buyers feel that they're intruding in your home.*

# What About Repairs?

Cosmetic repairs are important: sealing that small crack, replacing that missing tile, tightening that loose doorknob—and we recommend that you make all that are needed. Major repairs are a different story, however. You may think the roof only has a few good years left and replace the whole thing at big-time cost, but the buyer may have disagreed with you.

You might consider giving the buyer a chance to gauge these kinds of things themselves, unless major repairs are needed immediately, or for health reasons. Often, what happens is that if the buyer wants a repair done, the seller will offer a credit on the listing price instead. That'll save you time and, odds are, money.

Note that in some states, you'll also have to fill out a property disclosure that must be given to buyers, indicating what you know is wrong with the property. Your Realtor can help you with that, along with federally mandated disclosures such as the lead paint disclosure you'll need.

# Consider an Inspection

You might also consider a housing inspection; nearly all buyers will want one before they buy your house, and getting one done first can save you some surprises. Housing inspections are performed by professional inspectors (look under a heading such as "Home and Building Inspection Services" in the phone book).

# Choosing a Time of Year

Another part of preparing your house for sale is deciding when to sell it. Market activity is the highest starting March 1st and continuing to Memorial Day. The second highest is Labor Day to the week before Thanksgiving, but that's quite a bit reduced. Dead times include late summer and after Thanksgiving, when things are very dead, indeed.

# Question 8

# How Do I Best Market My House?

You've prepared your house for sale—now what about marketing it? This chapter digs into the actual process of marketing. If you're going FSBO, you should consider all these topics. Even if you're working with a Realtor, you should know about these topics to keep on top of the process (some Realtors are glad to have you help market your house; others aren't so accommodating).

Just about all houses that are sold sell through the techniques discussed in this chapter. Sometimes, a property is unique and will appeal only to a specialized audience, in which case you'll need specialized marketing—if you happen to own a $25-million estate in Maui, you might need the services of a marketing firm who will contact buyers in that range, advertise in estate magazines, and so on. But most sales can pursue a few effective techniques to find buyers, and we'll go into them here.

# Advertising

Advertising is the way to start, of course. If you're selling your house yourself, this task is up to you; if you're using an agent, it's up to them. Note that if you don't think you're getting enough exposure from your agent, ask if you can supplement her advertising efforts with some of your own—we've never known an agent who didn't want to save on their advertising budget. Just make sure your agent knows you're not trying to bypass her in working with buyers.

The most basic technique is the "For Sale" sign, which you can pick up at hardware or home improvement stores (make sure it is a two-sided sign that you can place perpendicular to the street). In a seller's market, that could be all you need; buyers will beat a path to your door. If you have a Realtor, they'll put the sign up for you. Make sure your sign says "For Sale," gives a contact phone number, and the real estate company's name, if you have one. You might also specify "By Appointment Only" if you want to make sure people call before knocking. Some people go so far as to put listing statements (coming up later in this chapter) in plastic holders on their signs so interested buyers can get more facts.

> *Note that if you don't think you're getting enough exposure from your agent, ask if you can supplement her advertising efforts with some of your own.*

As Realtors will tell you, calls recieved from people who've seen the sign (called *sign calls*) yield more sales than calls from ads (*ad calls*) because potential buyers have seen your house from the outside in its neighborhood and know what's being offered. Ad calls often come from people moving up and down columns of similar ads, so they're less likely to result in sales.

Classified ads are also important, especially if you're selling your house yourself. Use the standard abbreviations such as BR for bedroom, BA for bathroom, and so on, to save money—the cost of classified advertising mounts up quickly. To get an idea of how to write your ad, take a look at similar classified ads already in the paper, and always make sure you include the price if you don't want unqualified buyers to call you. Note also that, these days, many newspapers will automatically list your ad online, making it searchable from the Internet.

*If you're placing an add, read the paper for a week and see if there is a particular day that real estate ads proliferate. Be sure to place an add on this day.*

Real estate agents rarely use the classified ads, however, preferring instead to use real estate supplements in local papers. There are two reasons they usually do that: supplements are read by people expressly interested in buying real estate (who often don't even consider the classifieds), and supplement ads are often full-page ads taken out by the agency, showing many or all of their listings, which saves money for the agent. It's rare to see ads by individual sellers in the supplements, but it certainly does happen. If you have a Realtor, study your ad carefully for mistakes and overall tone. Don't be afraid to suggest improvements, but don't try to fine-tune too much—agents are human too, and if you try to run their business too much, you may find them becoming remote.

If you're placing a newspaper ad, read the paper for a week and see if there's a particular day that real estate ads proliferate (this often happens on the weekend). Be sure to place an ad on this day—buyers who've been shopping for a while know the "good" day to look for real estate listings and consequently will be more likely to spot your ad.

Beware of agents who promise truly grandiose marketing plans, because they often won't follow through. They might plan full-color brochures, special events, and so on. Be careful if it sounds too good to be true; they might be trying to buy your listing, as discussed in Question 6.

## The Multiple Listing Service

The Multiple Listing Service (MLS) is only available to member Realtors. We've already discussed this service; it lets Realtors list properties for sale in a computer-searchable way. You have access to the listings at *www.Realtor.com*. Some agencies still have big books of MLS listings that buyers can page through, but most search with a computer after getting an idea of what the buyer wants, and print out specific results. Your Realtor should be a member of the MLS and should list your house there.

If you're selling your house yourself, note that you can often find Realtors, especially discount brokers, who will list your house in the MLS for a fee, as mentioned in Question 4. If your FSBO house isn't selling rapidly, buying this service is a good idea.

## Computers and the Internet

More and more houses are being found online these days, through the MLS and other searchable sites. If you're good with computers, you might create your own Website for your house, so buyers can find it themselves or that you can direct them to. It costs very little to host a dozen internal and external photos of your house.

You can even use eBay to sell your house, but, as with all distance deals, be careful. EBay, for example, expects both buyers and sellers in its real estate transactions to follow through "in good faith" but offers little actual recourse if a deal turns sour. Some buyers buy houses sight unseen over the Internet, and if there are any major surprises or any suspicion you've misrepresented something, you could be in trouble. Authorities are cracking down on such issues more and more.

# Open Houses

A great way to market your house is to hold an *open house*. When buyers are in your house, it's much easier to make a sale. If you have a Realtor, he can arrange the open houses. Don't assume your Realtor will automatically schedule an open house for your property—you might have to ask im to set one up.

If you're planning an open house, make the house into as much of a showplace as you possibly can. Follow the tips in Question 7 to maximize both curb and interior appeal. If you're holding the open house yourself, be prepared to take down visitors' names and phone numbers when they arrive, and have a listing statement ready for buyers to take with them (see pg 56). If your Realtor will host the event, you should probably make other plans for the hours the house will be open and let the Realtor do his of her job. An anxious owner hovering around will send many potential buyers out the door before they've even had a chance to look around.

> *If you're planning an open house, make the house into as much of a showplace as you possibly can.*

As with showings, it's best to make things as easy for the Realtor as possible. The harder a house is to show, the less Realtors will show it. They may suggest putting a lockbox on a doorknob, for example, with a key inside so you don't have to meet them each him they want to show your house.

# Listing Statements

A *listing statement* is a marketing sheet to hand potential buyers when they come to see your house, making it easier for them to read up on your place later on. Listing statements usually include information about the number and dimensions of rooms, type of heat, lot size, and special features such as fireplaces, central air-conditioning, designer kitchen appliances, and so on. They're a good idea—you should leave a stack of them on a table if you have a Realtor so people can pick them up during showings. (How do you know if a planned showing actually happened while you were out? Realtors will leave a business card on a table if you're not there. Don't leave too many of those cards lying around—the competition can scare off some potential buyers, and others might wonder why the house hasn't sold yet if it's been shown so many times.) Be sure to include photos in your listing statement and list all the good points about your house—the things you want potential buyers to remember.

# Use Some Caution

When you advertise, beware of overstating what your house offers—these days, the buyer is getting more and more protection. You're probably going to have to fill out your state Seller's Disclosure statement in order to sell your house, and then you'll have to give a copy to the buyer. What happens if you say something misleading in your advertising—such as all wiring is less than 10 years old—and the buyer discovers some truly ancient stuff after moving in? You could be liable for the updating. If you're not sure, don't be too exact in your marketing (for example, say, "The roof is *approximately* 7 years old").

# Question 9

# Why Isn't My House Selling?

Perhaps you've put your house on the market and had a steady stream of prospective buyers—even an offer or two. Things are going as you expected. Great! You won't need this chapter; turn to the next one on how to handle offers. You're off and running.

On the other hand, if your house isn't generating offers as you'd expected, or if people just aren't coming back for second showings, you may have a problem. But don't worry, you can almost certainly fix it.

## What Are the Danger Signs?

If your house isn't generating any interest, if people just aren't showing up, even for open houses, then clearly you have a problem. Talk to your agent about what you might do differently. But if you're getting many showings and no offers, you also have a problem, although it might be harder to detect.

You might be showing the house frequently, but no one comes back for a second look. Or you might be getting only a few lowball offers from buyers who don't seem serious. All these are danger signs that something about the deal isn't doing what it should: attracting buyers.

# How Long Do I Have to Wait for an Offer?

How long you will have to wait depends on the market, of course. Sometimes, sellers get multiple offers, including some above asking price, within hours. Those are the conditions that sellers (but not necessarily buyers!) look forward to.

But in average markets, during the best selling times of the year, it's safe to say that if you haven't gotten any offers in six weeks, then there's a problem, and you should think about fixing it. Six weeks is not a hard-and-fast rule, however; if you're working with a Realtor, he will have a sure idea of how long it's taking houses to sell in your area.

> *If you haven't gotten any offers in six weeks, then there's a problem and you should think about fixing it.*

# If You Have a Problem, It Can Be Fixed

You can change some things about a house that might be slowing the sale, such as enhancing the house's appearance and fixing structural problems, as already discussed. New paint, clearing the yard, fixing wall cracks, adding new rugs—all those can do wonders. Sometimes, however, you can't fix a potential problem. The house's location, for example, or a nearby plant closing that's throwing everyone out of work and putting many houses on the market. (Living in the northeast, as we do, we've seen the latter happen far too often.)

In these cases, what you can change is the house's price. That's probably something you don't want to tamper with, but if your house isn't selling, you may not have much choice. So how do you set a new price?

# Discuss It With Your Agent

Real estate agents will say that any house can be sold—it's just a matter of setting the right price. Well, that may be true, but in serious down markets, following that advice may not get you a price you want to live with. Remember: If you don't have to sell, you can simply wait until the market improves.

If you're reluctant to lower the price, first consult with your agent about buyer's responses to your home. Ask your agent to contact other Realtors who have shown the home to get feedback about why their clients didn't make an offer. You might learn about a recurring problem that you can fix. Or you can consider other kinds of buyer incentives, such as offering to pay closing costs, a rent-to-own option, or seller financing.

But it's likely that you'll have to discuss a new price with your agent. In fact, because Realtors don't get paid if a house doesn't sell, they'll usually bring up the topic of a new price before sellers do. Typically, agents will suggest a 10 percent price reduction, rounded up to just below the next standard price boundary. For example, if your house is on the market for $149,000 and it's not selling, your agent may suggest deducting 10 percent, to give you $134,100, and then rounding up to just below the nearest $1,000 increment, making the new price $134,900. (Recall that you always want to set a price just below a standard price boundary such as this to make sure computerized searches don't miss your house because it's listed

$100 or so above the rounded figure that buyers may give to their agent.)

If you think chopping 10 percent off is too much, you're free to go with less. But bear in mind that there is such a thing as buyer fatigue—if buyers notice that your house has been on the market for a long time with no action, they may write it off, not even noticing that you've lowered the price.

> *Bear in mind that there is such a thing as buyer fatigue.*

You don't have to set a new price, of course. If you're willing to wait for your price, that's fine. We've seen FSBO buildings that have been for sale for years, and the seller never came down in price. Eventually, he got it. But most sellers don't have years to wait.

# After You've Set a New Price

When you've set a new price, make sure everyone knows it. This is important, because potential buyers may have seen your house and decided the price was too high—and those are exactly the people you have to reach.

If you're using a Realtor, make sure the listing indicates clearly and prominently that you're set a new price. Realtors often put text stripes across the corner of a house's picture saying something such as "New Price!" or "Price Reduced!" Houses with this kind of label always generate more interest—everyone loves a bargain.

If you've had interested potential buyers who didn't make an offer, tell them about the new price. If you're using a Realtor, do it through her.

# Once You've Set a New Price, You're Committed

Here's one thing to bear in mind: when you've set a new price to encourage buyers, you're committed to it. If you get offers based on the new price, it's very hard to increase that price again before signing with the buyer, although it can be done (as when there are multiple competing offers).

But if your agent is able to produce a "ready, willing, and able" buyer at the new price, you might have a hard time explaining if you want to turn them down. And you might be liable for the agent's commission if you can't explain. Be aware of this before you set and advertise a new price.

To sum this chapter up: if your house simply isn't selling, and if there's any kind of a market at all, the usual thing to do is to lower the price. That may not be something you're too happy about doing, but it's the advice you'll get from your Realtor— and if you want to sell your house in a reasonable amount of time, it may well be what you have to do.

# Question 10

## How Do I Handle Offers?

Getting a purchase agreement can be very exciting— someone wants to buy your house! There are plenty of ins and outs here, though, so Question 10 and 11 discuss how to handle purchase agreements and how to work with offers in general.

## Getting a Purchase Offer

When someone wants to buy your house, or to make an offer, that person will give you a purchase agreement, also called a purchase contract, or just a contract. (Realtors prefer to call them agreements, which sounds less threatening than contracts.) Usually, a purchase agreement comes through the buyer's Realtor. If you have a Realtor, it'll go to that Realtor, if not, it'll come to you directly.

Some agencies have standard purchase agreement forms that buyers fill out, with space left for the contingencies (special conditions that are to be fulfilled as a condition of the sale) that the buyer wants. Some buyers, however, write up their own purchase agreements.

Once it's been signed by the buyer and seller, a purchase agreement is a legally binding document, so we strongly recommend that you get your lawyer to look at the agreement before you sign anything. We always do.

The purchase agreement should give the exact location (including tax map number) and a description of the property. It should also clearly identify the buyer and the seller. The offered purchase price should be listed, as well as the method of payment (how much will be mortgaged, for example). The buyer should offer a deposit, called *earnest money*, to make you, the seller, know that this is a real offer. A typical amount is $1,000, deposited with the buyer's Realtor. (Theoretically, that money is yours if you sign the agreement and the buyer later reneges).

> *The purchase agreement should give the exact location (including tax number) and description of the property.*

Items fixed to the property, such as light fixtures on the walls, are normally taken to be included in the sale. If other items, such as stoves or refrigerators, will be included in the sale (this is called "conveying"), those conveyances should also be indicated in the agreement. The agreement should indicate the proposed closing date and how long the offer will last, typically a few days. Make sure the offer is signed and dated.

It's also normal to have a section listing contingencies, which are issues such as repairs that the buyer wants you to address; a clause about "adjustments," which refers to prorating utility bills or taxes that have already been paid; and a right-to-final-inspection clause, which says that the buyer is entitled to a final inspection just before closing. The final inspection clause is an important one; buyers can request this to make sure you've done any needed work. Study the wording of these clauses carefully—if worded badly, a final inspection clause can be a "weasel clause" that allows a buyer with cold feet to terminate the agreement at the last minute.

## What Are the Options?

When you receive an offer from a potential buyer, you have three options:

➲ You can sign the purchase agreement, indicating that you accept it as it stands without any changes.

➲ You can make a counter offer. To do this, cross out terms you don't accept and write in your own. A typical example is when the seller crosses out the buyer's price and writes in a higher one. Or you can write up a whole new contract, stating your terms.

➲ You can reject the offer with no further negotiation.

Most of the time, sellers make a counteroffer. As negotiations continue (see Question 12), it will become clear whether or not the buyer and seller can reach an agreement.

## Keep Your Cool

As discussed in Question 1, it's important to keep your cool and stay somewhat detached. You can only make conscious decisions if you're operating consciously. Selling is usually a waiting game, and it can be tempting to grab an offer when it appears. But no deal was ever made better by closing your eyes before leaping. Whether to accept or reject the offered price is up to you alone, of course, but when it comes to the rest of the agreement, it's time to invoke your team of real estate professionals, starting with your Realtor, if you have one.

## Go Over It With Your Realtor

An experienced Realtor has seen many purchase agreements, so the first step when you receive a written offer is to go over it with your agent. By law, your Realtor has to pass all offers on to you, but that doesn't make all offers worthy of your attention. Some might be so lowball, or demand so many changes, that you might reject them, flat out.

Realtors can go over the contract with you in depth, including what's there and also what's *not* there. For example, an offer somewhat below your hoped-for price but without any contingencies may be a good offer, because you'll save money on repairs other buyers might demand. Or, if the agreement is missing anything important, such as earnest money, your agent will probably find the problem at a glance.

But most Realtors aren't legal professionals, so it's also important to show the agreement to a qualified real estate lawyer. (Many brokers are also lawyers; in many states, attorneys can qualify for a broker's license more easily than other people can.) If you're selling the house without a Realtor, getting a lawyer's opinion of the purchase agreement is *essential*.

> *By law, your Realtor has to pass all offers on to you, but that doesn't make all offers worthy of your attention.*

## Getting a Good Lawyer

We strongly recommend that you get a real estate lawyer on your team. Real estate deals have so many potential legal snags that, unless you're an expert yourself, you should really have a lawyer. Don't sign any purchase agreement unless your lawyers okays it.

Finding a good lawyer is important; your Realtor, who has probably been involved in many closings, should be able to recommend several. Get the reasons for each recommendation, though—you don't want a lawyer who simply happens to be a pal of your Realtor. If you're not working with a Realtor, ask friends or colleagues who've been involved in a recent real estate transaction for their recommendations. Or you could always try the Yellow Pages—just be sure to get references from any lawyers you find this way.

Make sure you can get along well with the lawyer; interview candidates before choosing. Your lawyer should be:

- ➲ A specialist in real estate transactions.
- ➲ Able to handle escrow deals.
- ➲ Licensed to practice law in your area.
- ➲ Familiar with all your local codes and requirements.
- ➲ Reasonably priced.
- ➲ Accessible! If you can't get through after a couple of calls, don't use that lawyer.
- ➲ Able to handle things in a timely fashion. Watch out for someone who'll leave things to the last minute, which can postpone your closing.

Another question to ask: Will the lawyer handle court cases if necessary, or will he or she refer you to someone else? On the other hand, watch out for lawyers who turn to lawsuits too quickly because they like the fees involved. In real estate, such lawyers are called *deal breakers*.

To sum up: when you get an offer, keep your cool and go over it with your real estate team—your Realtor, if you have one, and your lawyer. Your team can advise you and point out problems. Ultimately, whether or not you accept an offer will be your decision. Sometimes, that decision is easy. But what if the offer is interesting but not perfect? That's where negotiation comes into play.

# Question 11

## How Do I Know the Buyer Is Real?

Buying a house is a big moment in people's lives, and many buyers turn out to be unready for it. Although no Realtor we know has kept statistics, a substantial fraction of offers never get to the closing stage simply because the buyer could not, or would not, carry through. An offer that fizzles out wastes your time, and it can damage the sale of your house if you have rejected other offers to accept one that didn't work out.

For that reason, it's worthwhile to consider the buyer before you accept an offer. After the closing, the buyer is usually much less of a concern to you because you have the money (unless, of course, you've given them a mortgage yourself) and you've transferred the property. But sometimes getting a buyer to the closing can be difficult, so, before you sign that purchase agreement, take a look at the topics in this chapter. Buyers often get cold feet—even after the sale, when it's called *buyer's remorse* (and you might end up fielding more phone calls from the buyer than you'd want). Question 11 is dedicated to deciphering just how ready, willing, and able the buyer really is.

# Dealing With the Buyer

If you're using a Realtor, it can be hard to communicate directly with the buyer. The Realtor is supposed to be your conduit to the buyer, but sometimes it can feel as though that conduit is plugged.

We've had deals in which the other party was very nervous and difficult to work with. In one such deal, the Realtor with whom we were working made things worse, changing our polite and warm questions to brisk and businesslike demands. The Realtor thought this more professional, and we only learned about this unfriendly, "businesslike" approach late in the deal. Our Realtor was literally stripping out all our "pleases" and "thank yous," as well as any personal touch or contact, which this particular buyer strongly needed for reassurance. We nearly lost the deal, and only a well-timed Christmas card expressing our thanks and appreciation sent from us directly to the buyer, saved it.

> *It is not an easy thing to dismiss your Realtor in the middle of negotiations because things can become sticky in terms of commissions and fees.*

Bypassing your Realtor to communicate with the buyer directly is usually an extreme measure. It is not an easy thing to dismiss your Realtor in the middle of negotiations because things can become very sticky in terms of commissions and fees. If you feel you're not getting through to the buyer or things are going too slowly, request a face-to-face meeting. Realtors may object, but if you believe that communication has become an issue, they can't refuse. If anything substantive is decided at such meetings, make sure you get it in writing right there—don't leave it verbal.

# Is the Buyer Motivated?

The first question has to do with the buyer's motivation. People just don't chassé out and buy a few houses for no reason. Finding out why the buyer wants to purchase a house can take you a long way toward determining a good candidate.

A buyer who is moving into the area or has already sold his or her old house has a valid motivation for buying your house. But a buyer who's out there "just testing the market," or one who wants to buy your house but hasn't even started the process of selling his or her own could be a problem.

# Does the Buyer Cooperate and Communicate?

Does the buyer appear interested and eager? If communication seems slow; if you're waiting for an answer and it's a long time coming, you could have a problem. Poor communication is a sign that the potential buyer is looking at other deals or is getting seriously cold feet. If you don't get answers or suspect that you can't work with the buyer, think about looking elsewhere.

# Is the Buyer Realistic?

Sometimes, buyers will offer deals that are too good to be true—20 percent over asking price, for example, with no competing buyer in sight. If the buyer is offering too good a deal, be careful; he or she may have little real drive to follow through.

Conversely, if you've gotten a real lowball offer—20 percent lower than you're asking or even less—the buyer may also not have a lot of drive to negotiate a price with which you can live. It can be a waste of time trying to bargain very low offers up to the reasonable range.

# Is the Buyer Willing to Put Down Earnest Money?

Purchase agreements usually come with "earnest money," a deposit of $1,000 or so to indicate the buyer's good faith. This money goes to you if the agreement is signed and the buyer ends up rejecting the deal for unsupportable reasons before closing. If that deposit isn't there, ask for it. If you can't get it, you've gotten a message from the buyer about his or her reliability.

# Does the Buyer Want to Wait an Overly Long Time Before Closing?

The buyer should have a time frame, and it should be explicit in the agreement. Closings are set typically one to three months after buyer and seller sign a purchase agreement, and the purchase agreement should give the suggested closing date. If the buyer wants to close later than three months down the road, it could be a sign of trouble. The buyer might want wiggle room or simply might not be really committed to the deal.

If the buyer sets a far-off closing date, find out the reason. When mortgage rates are low, backlogs can mean that lenders take a very long to time to approve loans. If that's why the buyer set a far-off closing date, that may be legitimate. Otherwise, remember that you have good reason to want to close the sale in a timely manner.

# Getting a Credit Check

You may want to check the buyer's credit as a practical test of his or her deal worthiness. For that, you'll need the buyer's permission (in writing) and Social Security number. Your Realtor may be able to help, or your bank if you're working with one. You can also do credit checks online. Search for "do a credit check" in a search engine such as Google.com.

You can also request a preapproval letter from the buyer's lender, of course, or ask if you can call the lender to find out the likelihood of loan approval. Note that there's a difference between prequalification, which simply reflects the lender's opinion based on borrower and lender, and preapproval, which is based on independent documentation and verified information. Preapproval is what you want to check.

Here's another thing to consider: Buyers sometimes ask for a "seller's concession," which is an amount added to the selling price and rebated later by the seller to the buyer. If the buyer asks for this, it could be a warning flag that he or she doesn't have enough money to go through with the deal. Make sure his or her bank has okayed the mortgage. Some banks don't allow seller's concessions because they amount to a bigger loan from the bank to the buyer.

## Are the Contingencies Realistic?

Ask yourself about the contingencies the buyer requests. If they want a new roof and siding but are unwilling to move accordingly on price, that's going to be a problem. As we'll discuss in the next chapter, you can offer the buyer credit for repairs you don't want to do. But if the buyer has unrealistic expectations, the situation is just the same as a lowball offer, and should be treated as such.

# $Q$*uestion* **12**

# How Do I Negotiate the Best Deal?

America is not really a nation of hagglers. In stores, prices are usually set and not open to bargaining. "You want fries with that?"

"Sure, but I'll only offer 59 cents."

That's not an exchange you're very likely to hear. But when it comes time to negotiate the best deal on selling a house, some haggling is going to be necessary.

Realtors can help here, having gone through the process many times already. They know the market, and they know what's going to be in a good offer. Note that, although Realtors can advise you on deals and communicate with the buyer, they're not supposed to argue prices up and down themselves. A Realtor can tell you his or her opinion of whether or not the deal is a good one, however.

Ultimately, okaying the deal will be up to you, so make sure you're getting the best deal you can.

# Is the Offer Reasonable?

A buyer who offers what you want and appears to be a good candidate makes things easy. Those deals do happen, of course, but often you'll have to weigh various factors and take a closer look.

Is the offer within 10 percent of the price of similar homes in the area? Are the contingencies reasonable? If so, you probably have a good offer. Sellers usually set their asking prices at amounts somewhat higher than what they'll settle for, so if you get one within 10 percent or so of your advertised price, that offer is worth considering.

Realtors can often size up deals quickly—remember, their job is to provide you with a "ready, willing, and able" buyer. If you turn down too many candidates that meet that description, you may be liable for commission charges from your Realtor.

# A Purchase Offer Is Not Just Price

Too many sellers get fixated on price and ignore the other parts of a deal, such as the contingencies the buyer wants. There are typically two types of contingencies: financial (where the deal is off if the buyer can't get a mortgage), and property fix-up (where the buyer requests repairs). A deal is made up of an entire package, and you have to consider everything together.

Is the buyer asking for seller financing, meaning that you'll take on a mortgage? Does the house require a lot of fixing up? Is the buyer asking for a seller's concession (see Question 11)? What other costs are there in the deal for you? It's extremely important to gauge the whole deal at once—don't look at the price alone.

# Negotiating Tips

Negotiating is an art—one that requires years to become proficient. So be prepared to spend some time and attention on the process. Keep your eyes open.

You can often determine your negotiating power based on how fast offers appear. If your house has been on the market for months and only one offer has come in, you might not be in the greatest selling position. In a hot market, on the other hand, you can say (for example) that you'll take offers next Monday between 9 a.m. and noon, and you might get a dozen. This puts you in a very strong position. If one offer doesn't look good, you can go with another.

When you're in a strong position, don't hesitate to take advantage. The worst the buyer can do is to say no to your counteroffer. If that happens, you can always try another counteroffer or another buyer.

Working with multiple offers can be great. If you're on the verge of rejecting someone's offer, first ask his or her Realtor if that buyer would be willing to match or exceed the currently leading offer.

Give on the small stuff, such as having some trim painted, or getting the sump pump serviced. Doing so can give you a surprising psychological advantage. Don't underrate this tactic; it's one we often use, and it can get big concessions.

> *You can often determine your negotiating power based on how fast offers appear.*

Don't be overly quick on replies, which can make you seem anxious. If you can't get what you want, let the deal cool for a few days. Just be sure you wait past the purchase offer's expiration date.

If there are other offers, a reasonable bargaining tactic is to make sure potential buyers know it; a little competition can do wonders to improve bids. Go through your Realtor on this. Be careful, though; as buyers, we've dealt with Realtors who continued to show a property even after we had a signed contract. The Realtor claimed to be looking for "backup offers"— but then used those offers to threaten us in negotiations. That kind of behavior is unethical and grounds for a complaint with the local board of Realtors. From a seller's point of view, a Realtor who threatens your potential buyer could ruin the whole deal.

Always keep in mind that the buyer is not your enemy. You're not trying to win a life-or-death power struggle; you're trying to come up with a deal that's acceptable to both parties.

> *Be careful. We've dealt with Realtors who continued to show a property even after we had a signed contract. The Realtor claimed to be looking for backup offers"—but then used those offers to threaten us in negotiations. This kind of behavior is unethical and grounds for a complaint with the local board of Realtors.*

# Negotiate Eye to Eye

This one is going to depend on your personal style, but some sellers find they can do better negotiating eye to eye, across a table. If you're working with them, have both Realtors attend. Negotiating this way isn't for everyone, but buyers often find it much easier to turn down a deal offered to them by your Realtor over the phone than to say no while sitting across from you.

# Don't Do Multiple Deals at Once

You may have multiple offers, but make sure you counter only one offer, then wait until you get a response. If you end up with multiple, simultaneous agreements to sell the same property, that's called multiple ratification and it's a bad problem. You could end up in court, sued by an unhappy potential buyer. (It is actually possible to put something in your purchase agreement to allow multiple ratifications, but that's very rare.)

If you have multiple offers, work with the one most attractive to you, and treat the others as backup offers; if the first deal falls through, pursue the next best backup offer.

# Making Counteroffers

In our experience, few purchase agreements are signed the first time; most go back and forth on price, contingencies, dates, and conveyances (such as refrigerators, stoves, and so on). When you make a counteroffer, be sure your reasons for rejecting the original offer are clear. Although it can be tempting, don't try to slip things past by changing the wording in parts of the agreement you think they'll miss— —the buyer's lawyer or Realtor will catch it. Any changes you make or new terms you specify in a counteroffer should be very clear.

Buyers may ask you for large-scale repairs that you're unwilling to make. If you're so inclined, you can offer a credit on the purchase price instead. You can credit the buyer for the full price of what such a repair might cost or split the difference.

In really bad markets, sellers sometimes offer to pay all or part of the buyer's closing costs. This is better for the buyer's cash situation, because the typical buyer only puts down 20 percent or less of the selling price. So, if you reduce the price, they'll only benefit by 20 percent of that reduction. But be careful: closing costs can easily run to $8,000 or more, so make sure you know to what you're agreeing.

# Question 13

## Will It Pass an Inspection?

All prudent buyers are going to have your house inspected before closing. You'll usually find something about a housing inspection built into the purchase agreement, often saying that the inspection will be done within 10 days of signing. After the inspection has been done, the buyer will typically come to you with a list of requested repairs. Purchase agreements are usually written so that you don't have to make the repairs if you don't want to—you can declare the agreement void, you can make the repairs, or offer a credit.

Because the buyer will almost certainly have your house inspected, it's worth knowing what an inspector will look for. That's the subject of this chapter, which contains a number of items that inspectors check, starting with the grounds, to the roof, to the interior.

# Wet Areas

Inspectors usually begin by walking around the property, noting such items as poor drainage in the yard. Does your property have any long-standing wet spots? You might want to take care of them before the inspector comes.

# Siding

The inspector will check the outside of the house, such as the condition of the siding. If you've got an older type of siding, such as asbestos tile, he'll note it as such. Asbestos tile is usually not a big issue, but the buyer will have to be notified.

# Roof

Any inspector worth his salt will climb up on the roof for a detailed look. The inspector will note the condition of the roof, any missing shingles, how many layers of shingles there are, cracked roof coverings, and so on.

# Gutters

Inspectors are often big on suggesting gutters if a house doesn't have them. Without gutters, water falls directly from the roof to the foundation area and sits there, possibly going directly into the foundation. For long-term foundation protection, gutters are a good idea, and if you don't have them, the inspector might suggest the buyer ask for them.

# Chimney

Chimney inspection is a routine part of housing inspections; we've found many a chimney with internal cave-ins (posing carbon monoxide risks). Some inspectors even have TV cameras they can lower into chimneys. Also watch for vines that go into the chimney or near it's top—those could be fire hazards, and at the very least, vines that go into a chimney can become highways for insects.

## Ceiling Wet Spots

Inside the house, inspectors will notice any wet spots in the ceiling. If you have any, and the cause has been removed, re-touch the paint.

## Clogged Pipes

In older houses, the inspector might run the taps while flushing the toilet to gauge water flow; if it slows dramatically, your pipes might be filled with scale. Inspectors also frequently check to see whether sinks have been vented for proper drainage.

## Wiring

How's your wiring? Is it up to code? Inspectors will not only check wiring in the basement they'll typically lift drop ceilings to take a look.

## Dry Rot and Termites

As you can imagine, dry rot and termite damage, especially in joists, is a big problem. If the damage is evident, the inspector will tell the buyer; if it's suspected, the inspector may suggest a specialized inspection.

## Pipes

Is your plumbing lead (not good)? Galvanized? Copper? What parts are plastic? All that will be noted.

## Wet Basement

Does your basement flood? Are there water lines? If you have a sump pump, is it unusually large, or do you have two of them? The inspector will pay special attention to water damage to any wooden posts or support members.

## Water Heater and Furnace Venting

Inspectors check the age and condition of furnaces and whether or not they're properly vented, as well as the condition of filters. An inspector might use a match, a candle, or a detector, for example, to check whether carbon monoxide is being properly vented.

## Asbestos

Asbestos is a mineral fiber that, in the past, was used for insulation. Inhaling high levels of asbestos fibers can damage the lungs or cause cancer, so inspectors are careful to look for asbestos problems in older homes. Are your furnace and pipes wrapped in asbestos? If so, the inspector might recommend encapsulating the asbestos or even removing it and replacing it with another type of insulation.

## Radon

Radon is a colorless, odorless radioactive gas that occurs naturally in soil and rock and can sometimes infiltrate homes. It's also sometimes found in well water and some building materials. High levels of radon can cause health problems, including cancer, so many buyers will check radon levels as part of the home inspection. Inspectors perform radon checks by placing a detector in the basement or other low-lying area and returning for it three days later.

# Mold

Toxic mold growing inside a building is another potential source of health problems. Checking for mold, especially black mold (which can cause respiratory ailments), is becoming increasingly popular. If you think your house might have mold problems, it's a good idea to have it checked out and possibly fixed (see "Mold Inspection and Remediation" in the phone book). Mold inspections are optional, but many buyers will want them.

# Foundation

The inspector will also note foundation cracks and settling. Like mold, foundation problems can scare many buyers, so you might want to address this before a potential buyer conducts an inspection, if that's workable for you.

# Finding Inspectors

The previously mentioned items are not an exhaustive list of what an inspector will check, of course. There are literally thousands of items that can come to the attention of an inspector. If you want to head off serious problems, you might get your own inspection done first (look for "Building Inspection Services" or "Home Inspection Services" in the phone book). An inspection will typically run $200 to $500.

The American Society of Home Inspectors (ASHI) is a professional organization of inspectors, to which you might ask prospective inspectors if they belong. Joining isn't easy, however—an inspector must have done at least 250 inspections and pass two written exams. Call 800.743.2744 or go to *www.ashi.com* for more information.

Also, ask whether the inspector is fulltime, how many inspections he or she performs annually, and whether he or she has any special certificates or licenses. Get a cost estimate before starting. You can also ask if the inspector is bonded (giving you protection in case of accidents) or carries errors-and-omission insurance (client protection in case the inspector misses something). And it never hurts to ask for references.

# $Q$*uestion* **14**

# What's Escrow All About?

Let's say you've signed the purchase agreement with the buyer. What next? There's a lot of money involved in deals such as yours, and before that money starts getting thrown around, you should know the process set up for handling it. That process is called *escrow*. It's the very backbone of the whole the deal.

Your lawyer may handle the details of setting up and handling escrow for you. Even so, it's worth learning what's in this chapter so you know the details of what's going on with the money.

## What Is Escrow?

When the deal is signed (called *ratification*), buyer and seller may well prefer someone they can both trust to hold the stakes while the rest of the deal is worked out (such as handling contingencies in the agreement).

An escrow functions as neutral territory, involving trustworthy third-party people who can hold and handle not only the money involved, but the documents related to the sale as well. These funds and documents are released at the closing. Escrow ensures that nothing changes hands—no money, no title or deed—until all the conditions of the sale have been met.

# How Does It Work?

Here's how escrow usually works: On the next business day after signing the agreement, you or the buyer (or a Realtor or lawyer for either one or both) opens an escrow with a neutral third party.

The person or agency that holds the money and/or documents in escrow is called the *escrow holder* or *escrow officer*. They'll hold those items related to the deal in a way that makes sure there will be no allegations of cheating, and, hopefully, fewer misunderstandings.

# Get Your Lawyer Involved

An escrow holder is typically a lawyer, a bank, a title company, or even a company that specializes in escrows.

You can get your Realtor's recommendation on who to use for the escrow. Because he has been involved in many deals like yours, he'll know who's good to work with.

You may, of course, use or disregard your Realtor's advice on escrow holders, but we recommend that you get your lawyer involved, preferably before you and the buyer settle on an escrow holder. Make sure your lawyer understands and agrees to any escrow agreements, and, if necessary, make sure you get everything in writing. Your lawyer will help protect your interests here. A reasonably fast response from your lawyer will be good for both you and the buyer, and it's another reason getting an accessible lawyer is important.

# What's an Encumbrance?

One of the things that escrow officers deal with is *encumbrances*. An encumbrance is another person's or agency's (such as a corporation) claim on your property. Financial encumbrances, called *liens*, are all about using your property to secure a debt, and that might be a first mortgage, a second mortgage, property tax liens, state tax liens, or a lien made against your property by a workman who claims you didn't pay him. Liens are recorded in the County Recorder's office and can be researched there.

There are other types of liens that can restrict the use or sale of your property called *easements*. These are usually recorded in your deed, such as the right of a power company to run lines across or under your property, or of the city to use part of your land adjoining the street for expansion, and so on. Easements might even say that you can't obstruct someone else's view of a lake; it all depends on what's in the deed. These are the kinds of items that escrow officers will have to deal with to make sure your deal conforms with what's legal.

> *Financial encumberances, called* liens, *are all about using your property to secure a debt.*

# What Does the Escrow Officer Do?

Buyers put money into an escrow in order to make sure the process goes smoothly, all the way through obtaining the title. You're on the opposite side of the equation; you're getting the money by giving the buyer the title. Escrow officers handle the down-and-dirty details of this process. What they actually do varies from state to state, but the following is a general outline.

89

Usually, after escrow is started, the escrow officer orders a title search of your property from a title company. Both you and the buyer will get a preliminary report on who owns the property (also called a *prelim*). This report also indicates encumbrances that limit the free use of your property, such as loans or easements. Note that it's possible that the buyers will cancel a deal if the prelim indicates serious encumbrances about which they didn't know.

> *Make sure that the escrow officer is instructed not to transfer title until you're satisfied that the deal is complete, and that you and your lawyer are convinced that all your requirements have been met.*

The escrow officer also holds funds and makes payouts. When the escrow is closed, the escrow officer uses the funds in escrow to pay parties that need to be paid, which can include paying off any loans you have on the property. When paying out money, the escrow officer may need to notify the government of the money you're getting.

Escrow officers also typically prepare and record documents, such as a grant deed that you sign to transfer title to the buyer. And the escrow officer records the deed when the escrow closes. Make sure, of course, that the escrow officer is instructed not to transfer title until you're satisfied that the deal is complete, and that you and your lawyer are convinced that all your requirements have been met.

Escrow officers can also get payoff information on mortgages, loans, and other liens that might be on your property. They'll ask you for a list of lenders that might have an interest in the sale of your property. It'll help, and save you time, if you can provide them with, for example, the latest copy of a monthly mortgage statement, property tax bill, utility bills, and so on, as they ask for them.

Escrow officers can also create both estimated and final closing statements. These statements provide you with an overview of where the money is going in the deal, and they'll have many items that, unless you've had experience with closings, will be a total mystery. Make sure you go over them in detail with your escrow officer or lawyer. It's very important that you understand what all the (many) charges are that will be made on the funds in escrow. Question 16 tells you more about closing statements.

# Question 15

## How Do I Get Ready for Closing?

It's time to schedule the big day— closing. Everything's been agreed to, you've been able to satisfy the contingencies in the purchase agreement (finally fixing that crack in the bedroom wall that you've lived with for years), and the buyer got his mortgage. Now it's time to set up the closing.

If it's any comfort, the buyer will usually be doing more than you will—setting up hazard insurance, title insurance, the mortgage; handling closing costs; and more. But there's still much for you to do to prepare.

## Scheduling the Closing

The first thing to do is to schedule the closing, usually done by one party's lawyer or the escrow officer. Closings are often held at an office of the lending institution. The closing date may be set in the purchase agreement, but it's usually the banks and lawyers that set the final date.

Because the buyer has a lot more to do at the closing than you do, the buyer is often requested to come earlier than you to start the process.

When you set the date, be careful about scheduling a closing just before the end of the year or just after it. There are all kinds of possible pitfalls here, such as taxes (you might not want to close next year, for example, because of what it'll do to your capital gains taxes) and other year-long expenses. The holidays also seem to drain a lot of energy from people, and it's notoriously hard to keep a closing anywhere near the end of the year on schedule.

*Because the buyer has a lot more to do at the closing than you do, the buyer is often requested to come earlier than you to start the process.*

## Stay in Touch With the Escrow Officer

Keep communication going with the escrow officer; if that's your lawyer, be sure to stay in good contact. Closings often involve many people, and even more documents, and getting together all that's needed is a big job—one that often isn't done quite right, forcing a postponement when a document is missing.

So if you haven't heard from the escrow officer for a while, contact him to make sure things are okay and proceeding as they should. Ask if there are any documents you should be supplying, and whether he has gotten all they need from the buyer's lawyer.

## Getting a Survey

In some states, you'll be required to perform a survey. Lending institutions often require this to make sure that what they're helping to buy is what they've been told is being bought.

Be aware that surveys can often come up with some surprises, even disagreeing with previous surveys. So, if you need one, get it done early in the process. For example, your neighbor's fence may turn out to be on your property, and the lender will require that you have your neighbor sign documents indicating that he won't contest changes to the fence. If the survey does show any problems, these will have to be resolved before the deal can close.

## Getting Loan Payoff Statements

Ask the escrow officer to order all needed loan payoff statements and/or forms for you at once, such as those needed to pay off your mortgage. These can be a long time coming, so the sooner they're ordered, the better.

## Getting the Estimated Closing Statement

The escrow officer should also be able to provide you with an estimated closing statement, giving you an overview of the cash flow during the closing. There's usually a lot going on here, so make sure you understand where all the money is going. There will be a lot deducted from the actual amount you receive, so ask a lot of questions.

## Handling the Final Inspection

The buyer will typically request a final inspection of your house just before closing (this is usually listed in the purchase agreement). This is the buyer's last chance to make sure all the changes he wants have been performed.

If not, there could be a dispute, and the buyer may even want to cancel the purchase agreement. You don't want that to happen, so coordinate with the buyer on any major repairs before the last minute. Good communication throughout the process is one of the best ways to avoid last-minute problems. Also, don't forget that fixtures (items fixed to the house, such as ceiling fans and shutters) conveyed to the buyer unless otherwise specified in the purchase agreement, so don't remove any fixtures that the buyer is expecting.

# Handling Utilities

You should also cancel utility service for the day you move out or on the closing date when the buyer takes possession. Utility bills will be pro-rated and settled at the closing.

If you're closing when it's freezing outside, don't turn off the heat, but do ask the utility company for a reading on the closing date or shortly before so the heating bill can be pro-rated and paid at closing.

# Watch That Closing Date

Closing dates have a way of slipping. If that's not a big problem for you, then when it happens you won't be dismayed. In our experience, you have to ride some lawyers to make sure they do what they need to do, including sending documents to the other side's lawyer in time.

Parenthetically, the buyer often has a big incentive to make sure the closing isn't delayed—when asking for a fixed-rate loan, a buyer can lock in the rate for up to 60 days or so. If the closing is pushed back too far, the lender will often add a quarter point (that is, .25 percent) to the mortgage rate.

# Bring Your Checkbook

Here's another thing to do to prepare for the closing: bring your checkbook. That surprises many sellers, because they think, not unreasonably, that they're the ones who will get paid at the closing. But closings are complicated things, and cash flows in several directions. Last-minute adjustments are often required, such as those that involve pro-rating utility and tax bills. Because the final closing statement will already have been printed, the lawyers may ask you to make these last-minute adjustments with a check to the buyer.

# Question 16

What Happens at Closing?

It's the big day at last— closing. This is the day on which the deal is done, and your house changes hands. You arrive with the keys and leave with a check. The buyer usually, but not always, takes possession of the house at closing; what actually happens should be specified in the purchase agreement. There are all kinds of possibilities, even a rent-back situation in which the seller stays in the house and pays the buyer rent for a specified period.

So what can you expect at closing? What happens? It's complicated (but typically less complicated for you than for the buyer). We'll walk you through the process in Question 16, but also take a look at Question 17, where we discuss the documents that are signed at a closing.

## Handling the Jitters

You may feel jittery before the closing and be subject to *seller's remorse*. You may have heard about buyer's remorse—

the buyer's regret and doubts about buying a house—but seller's remorse is just as real. Seller's remorse can be the conviction that you're selling for much less than you should or that you're otherwise making a bad deal. It can also hit with realization that you're going to have to say goodbye to your house. It really is true—you walk into the closing with the keys to your house and leave without them.

Be prepared for the jitters, and face the issues early. Also, see Question 1 for more on the emotional aspects of selling a house.

## Who Will Be There?

Closings can involve a large cast of characters or they can involve just a few people. Here are some of the people you may see. You and the buyer, of course, are the principals at the closing. You both will probably also have lawyers there, and the escrow officer will be there. The lending institution typically has a lawyer at the closing as well.

Besides these people, the lending institution's loan officer may attend, as well as any Realtors involved (this is when they collect their commissions).

## The Steps

Exactly how your closing will work is up to your state's laws. The whole plan here is that the buyer will receive marketable title to your property and you will receive the purchase price (minus the inevitable deductions). Although the details vary from state to state, here are the steps that you'll see.

By the time you get to the closing, the buyer may have already been there for half an hour or so, signing documents and setting up the mortgage. The escrow agent or your lawyer should verbally go over the process with you as things happen, giving you an indication of the money owed you by the buyer, such as prepaid taxes, or what you owe the buyer, such as unpaid taxes. This data will all appear in the closing statement.

You'll provide proof of inspection and any necessary repairs, unless this step has already been handled.

The buyer will complete signing all mortgage documents, obligating him to repay his loan based on the house as security. They'll also hand over a certified check (or in rare cases, a personal check) to the escrow officer for the balance of the down payment, as well as personal checks for any needed adjustments.

Here's the big moment—the escrow officer then gives the buyer the title to the house as a signed deed (also called a *warranty deed*). This is not the actual full deed, which lists the entire history of the property—that will be sent to the buyer by the escrow officer some weeks after the closing. The deed, of course, is the most important document involved in the closing.

The escrow officer then gives you the purchase price minus deductions as listed in the closing statement (such as tax or monthly utility adjustments). This is usually a check or a confirmation of funds wired to an account.

> *You'll provide proof of inspection and any necessary repairs, unless this step had already been handled.*

If you have a mortgage on the house that you need to pay off, the escrow officer or your lawyer will receive the funds in trust to pay off the mortgage on the date of closing. (Your escrow officer will already have obtained payoff information from your lender.) At or soon after closing, you'll also owe any Realtor commissions, lawyer's fees, and some taxes.

Both you and the buyer will get a closing statement, called a HUD 1 statement. This will show all the cash flow that's happened at the closing, including such items as lawyer's fees, Realtor commissions, prepaid or unpaid property taxes, prepaid interest on the mortgage, recording fees, title insurance, document preparation fees, transfer tax, mortgage tax (for some states), and so on. The buyer usually pays the closing costs, and you usually pay the Realtors' commissions, which are usually handed to the Realtors directly at closing.

Both you and the buyer sign the HUD 1 form, the closing statement. This is a paper trail of what's gone on during the closing. By signing it, you agree that the dollar amounts entered are correct (although it's not uncommon for small adjustments to be made afterwards when lawyers review the HUD 1).

The expenses that appear on this form will be listed as credits or debits to you or the buyer. Keep this document at all costs; it's your record of the transaction. You should also ask for a copy of all documents you sign at the closing.

And that's the process. For more details, take a look at the Question 17, where we discuss the actual documents signed at closings.

Now it's done. It's time to hand over the keys.

# Handing Over the Keys

The keys to the property are usually handed over to the buyer at closing. The keys probably won't be in service long, because it's customary to change the locks on the house after closing. Besides the keys, you should also hand over any garage door openers and security remotes.

> *The keys to the property are usually haded over to the buyer at closing.*

# Recording the Documents

The last part of the closing is the recording process. Many of the legal documents, such as the warranty deed, have to be recorded, and the fact of the sale itself must be recorded. The escrow officer or lawyer will handle the recording process for you (the recording fees will appear in the closing statement).

This step usually takes place right after the closing, at offices such as the county clerk's office.

# Handling Delays

Because closings involve the coming together of a number of very busy people, they're often subject to delays. On occasion, even one of the principals, such as you or the buyer, can't attend. The missing person can address this issue by giving someone the power of attorney to sign for them, or papers can be presigned before the closing.

Although we've been in situations where the lawyers suggested power-of-attorney for the missing party, we've always held out for an in-person signing. Although power-of-attorney signatures are legal, they introduce another level of complication and may be subject to challenges. Sometimes you can't avoid them but, if you can, we recommend that you do.

# Resolving Disputes

Last-minute disputes can flare up at closings, often over whether or not a piece of personal property (such as the refrigerator or the dining-room curtains) is included in the sale. We've heard of closings that have become real circuses. When a problem arises is when a good escrow officer can be invaluable, saving the deal by calmly reminding both parties of the terms to which they agreed—another reminder to make sure you choose your escrow officer carefully.

# Question 17

## What Gets Signed at Closing?

There are plenty of documents to sign at closing, and what actually happens at your closing depends on your deal and your state. But to help clarify the miasma of paperwork, we'll go over some of the documents that can appear at closings. Note that it's likely that some of these won't appear at your closing, and some others not listed here might appear! That's because laws and requirements vary from state to state.

To give you the full closing picture, we're going to go over documents signed by you and also those signed by the buyer, so you know what's going on as all that paper's flying around.

## Promissory Note

This one is signed by the buyer, and it's the agreement between the buyer and the lending institution, detailing the terms of the loan. All the loan data are here, including the amount of the loan, the interest rate, payoff terms, length of the loan, and so on. You can think of it as the IOU signed by the buyer.

# Monthly Payment Document

This one is signed by the buyer. It details the total monthly payment she'll be paying the lender. It gives all the information on payments and itemizes how much of each payment goes toward principal, taxes, insurance, escrow items, and interest.

# Truth-in-Lending Statement

This one is signed by the buyer. The Truth-in-Lending statement is also called Regulation Z, and it shows the amount financed and the complete cost of the loan over its entire term. It also lists explicitly the annual percentage rate (APR) of the loan. This document is created so the buyer understands and agrees to exactly what she's getting into.

# The Mortgage

This one is signed by the buyer. The mortgage itself is a lien against the property. This document is what sets up the lien and lets the lending institution foreclose on the property if the buyer goes into default.

# Itemization of Amount Financed

This one is signed by the buyer. This document lists any prepaid finance costs mentioned in the Truth-in-Lending statement. These costs will be deducted from the loan amount given to the buyer by the lending institution.

# HUD 1 Closing Statement

This is the closing statement, and it's signed by both you and the buyer. This document details the entire cash flow of the deal. It shows all the money you get from the buyer, the closing costs, and the adjustments for items you've paid ahead or still owe, such as taxes or utility bills, loan fees, Realtor commissions, and so on. Some of the charges involved in the deal may already have been paid, such as survey or appraisal fees, in which case they may be listed as "POC" (paid outside of closing).

This document is required by Federal law, and it's filled in by the escrow officer. Make sure you keep a copy for your records; your lawyer, the buyer, the lending institution, and the escrow officer should all keep copies, as well.

## Warranty Deed

This is signed by you. This is the actual document that transfers the title of the property from you to the buyer. The escrow officer will usually prepare this for you, and, as you already know, it's the most important document at the closing.

## Tax Proration Agreement

Signed by you and the buyer. Property taxes can be difficult to figure because next year's actual tax rate may not be known. This is an agreement between you and the buyer to prorate taxes when it's known what's owed. Usually, this document is only invoked when there's a big change in the property taxes.

## Homeowner's Dues Proration Agreement

This one is signed by you and the buyer. This document is all about prorating homeowner's dues, if there are any, such as those that are due to a condominium association.

## Name Affidavit

This one is signed by you and the buyer. This is a slightly odd document, but it usually comes up at closing. It certifies that the names you and the buyer use at closing are your legal names. If either of you has a former name or has performed business using another name, this affidavit makes that explicit.

# Borrower's Affidavit

This one is signed by the buyer. In it, the buyer certifies, to the lending institution's satisfaction, that the buyer has not changed the property in any way that might cause a problem with the title.

# Seller's Affidavit

This one is signed by you. Similar to the borrower's affidavit, it certifies that you have not changed the property in any way that might cause a problem with the title.

# Acknowledgment of Survey and Termite Reports

This one is signed by the buyer. It certifies that the buyer approves of the survey and termite reports, if applicable. This document doesn't always appear at closings, even if there have been surveys and termite reports.

# 1099 Form

This one is signed by you. It's an Internal Revenue Service form in which you report the proceeds from the deal for tax purposes. Unfortunate, but required.

# Confirmation of Payoff

This one is signed by you. It's a document that shows where the funds paid by you to satisfy liens actually go.

# Compliance Agreement

This one is signed by both you and the buyer. This document certifies that, if there are any typographical errors in any of the closing documents, you both will cooperate to correct and accept changes. Because closings are so complex and involve so much money, this document has become standard. You can probably imagine the kinds of typos it was designed to address (imagine finding that you're suddenly owed one-tenth the amount you thought you should get because of a slipped decimal place).

# Question 18

## What About Taxes?

The closing is over, and the new owners are moving into the house. At last, the whole process—dealing with Realtors, potential buyers trooping through the house, the lawyers, and the bankers—is over. Or is it?

Don't put everything behind you just yet, because there may still be tax repercussions from the sale. The IRS and various state tax agencies may assess taxes on any profits you made from the deal. And that's what this Question 18 is about. In particular, we're going to discuss capital gains taxes.

Note that we just present guidelines here, not legally-binding tax advice—for that, you need to go to a tax advisor. This chapter is meant to help you to get you familiar with an overview of the tax situation and is no substitute for real legal advice, especially because the tax situation changes frequently.

# What Was the Profit?

The profit you made on a house deal comes from the price you sold it for minus the price you paid for it. The difference between those two prices may come from many factors, such as improvements you made to the house, the rise of the market, and so on. As far as the IRS is concerned, not all profits are the same; profit due to the improvements you made isn't potentially taxable. For example, if you bought your house for $100,000, made $10,000 worth of improvements, and then sold it for $200,000, the taxable gain would only be

$$\$200,000 - \$100,000 - \$10,000 = \$90,000.$$

So how do you figure the profit for tax purposes? Start with the money you received for the sale. The IRS lets you deduct some costs associated with the sale, such as lawyer fees, title fees, escrow fees, advertising fees, Realtor commissions, recording fees, and so on. Then you need to subtract the *cost basis* of your house.

The cost basis begins with the price you paid for your house, and you can often include some closing and escrow costs that you paid. That makes sense—they're costs associated with the deal that you originally made to purchase your house, and you shouldn't be taxed on them.

After that, you add the verifiable costs of improvements you made to the house to the cost basis. An improvement is something that increases the value of your house or prolongs its useful life. For example, adding central air conditioning is considered an improvement, as would the addition of a new sun room or other rooms, a pool, landscaping, and so forth.

You can add the value of such improvements directly to your cost basis, dollar for dollar.

However, repairs that keep your house in livable condition are *not* considered improvements. These include repairs such as fixing a leaking water heater or broken panes of glass, repainting worn areas, filling in holes, and so on. Do not add the cost of these items to the cost basis.

Note that it can be a fine line here—what's an improvement and what's a repair? If you're in doubt, consult a tax advisor.

Other things can affect the cost basis as well, such as deductions you may have taken if you treated all or part of the property as rental or business property. Again, if such issues apply to your situation, check with a competent tax advisor.

After you've calculated how much you made from the sale, subtract the cost basis to determine how much potentially taxable profit you've made. The IRS already knows about your sale because of the 1099 you filed at the closing, but you may also need to report the sale the next time you file Federal taxes, using a Schedule D form.

After you've calculated the profit from the sale, will all that profit be taxable? Not necessarily. See the next section.

# How Much Is Taxable?

The relatively new rules for figuring taxable gains on sales made after May 6, 1997, give most homeowners great exemptions from taxes after house sales. (Note, of course, that the national tax code is revised frequently and these rules can change without warning.)

Here's the current rule: As long as the property was owned and used as your principal residence for at least two of the five years before the sale, married couples can exclude up to $500,000 from taxation, and singles up to $250,000.

*The IRS already knows about your sale because of the 1099 you filed at the closing, but you may also need to report the sale the next time you file Federal taxes, using a schedule D form.*

In the previous example, where you bought your house for $100,000, made $10,000 worth of improvements, and sold it for $200,000, your profit is $90,000. That's well below the exclusion limits, whether you're married or not.

On the other hand, say that you bought the house for $400,000, put $50,000 of improvements into it, and sold it for $800,000. In that case, you've made a profit of

$$\$800,000 - \$400,000 - \$50,000 = \$350,000.$$

If you're married, that's under the $500,000 limit, but if you're single, you could owe taxes on the amount over the $250,000 exclusion; in this case, you'd owe taxes on $100,000.

## Other Taxes, Too

Besides the IRS, states also collect taxes on income and capital gains, so you may owe tax there, too. Those rules are going to vary state by state, of course.

Fortunately, most states use the same capital gains exclusion rules as the IRS does—that is, married couples can exclude up to $500,000, and singles up to $250,000. So, if you owe capital gains taxes to the IRS, you probably owe them to your state as well. But the good news is that most sellers fall under the exclusion limits and, therefore, don't owe taxes on the proceeds of the sale.

# Question 19

# What About Moving?

Unless you've made other arrangements in the purchase agreement, you've got to be out when the buyer takes possession, usually at closing. This chapter discusses the moving process, which you should start thinking about at least four to six weeks before the actual move. Moving is not something you want to have to worry about during the chaos leading up to closing.

There are plenty of questions to ask here. Do you want to move everything yourself? Do you want to sell or donate some items first (eBay, garage sales, and so on)? If you want to use a mover, do you want the mover to pack—and unpack? What about moving insurance?

## How Do You Want to Move?

You can save a lot of money by moving yourself, but it's going to be a lot more work. Whether you want to save your money or your time is a decision only you can make. Most homeowners we know who've sold their houses use movers, because homeowners typically have been in their houses for longer than renters and have more to move.

If you're doing the move yourself, you might want to rent a truck or a trailer. Check in the phone book under "Truck Renting and Leasing." Truck sizes range from 10 feet, which will hold the contents of a small apartment, to 24 feet, which you'll probably need for a four-bedroom house. It's usually more expensive to rent one-way than it is to return the vehicle to the location you rented it from. You'll also have to acquire boxes and other moving supplies. Many truck rental companies also sell these, or an Internet search for "Moving Supplies" will find you direct suppliers of boxes and moving kits.

If you want to go with a mover, you have many options from which to choose. Do you want the movers to pack your belongings, or will you do it? (You can also pack some items and let the movers pack the rest.) Do you want the movers to unpack your belongings, at an extra charge? How much insurance do you want? The answers to these questions probably depend on the price of these services, and that depends on which mover you choose.

## Choosing a Mover

You've probably got a good selection of movers from which to choose; take a look at the "Movers" section in the phone book. Nearly all movers will walk through your house on request and give you a free estimate. Moves that are fewer than 50 or 100 miles (depending on the mover) are usually priced by the hour. For more distant moves, estimates are based on the weight of what you're moving.

There are three types of estimates:

➲ **Binding estimates** are guaranteed prices, sometimes with a few hundred dollars' wiggle room, as listed on the estimate.

⊃ **Non-binding estimates** are just that: non-binding. Be careful of this kind of estimate, because it really means nothing. Some movers will give you a lowball estimate, only to sting you on the final bill.

⊃ **Not-to-exceed estimates** give you a cap on the moving costs. Theoretically, if the move costs less, you pay less.

As you might imagine, we recommend that you request a binding or not-to-exceed estimate; too many people have gotten a big, unpleasant surprise after agreeing to a non-binding estimate. Get estimates from several movers; sometimes movers already have fairly full schedules and will give you a high estimate to see if you'll bite. Don't be shy about saying that you received a lower estimate from a competitor. And get the estimate in writing and make sure it's signed.

Getting estimates isn't all you should do. Ask movers for references from people who've moved with them in the past and for documentation of their service history. Ask also if they're bonded or insured; some local movers aren't.

When you choose a mover, you'll get a service order: a signed form that details what services you want from the mover, and when. Check the service order over carefully and make sure it's what you've ordered.

You'll probably want some form of insurance to cover your belongings, which the mover should provide. Most movers' basic insurance insures your items by the pound but you'll want better insurance than that. Make sure the cost of insurance is included in the estimate, and know what the deductible is. Your homeowner's insurance may cover your belongings during a move—contact your insurance agent to find out.

If you get insurance, be absolutely certain you do all that's needed to activate the insurance. This can include making sure that the moving company has specified (and initialed, if necessary) the insurance you want on the service order and signing off various forms on loading day, including one that indicates you approve of the shipment and its condition. The mover may seal the truck with plastic tags, for example, and ask you to sign that the shipment was satisfactorily loaded. Be careful about insurance—we've known too many people who moved thinking that their possessions were insured when they actually weren't because the service order insurance options weren't marked and signed.

## Setting a Date

You'll need to set the dates for your move with the mover. If you want the mover to pack your stuff first, the movers will typically pack one day, then load the next. The service order you sign will list all the dates, including the unloading date, which the mover will set. Keep in mind that you're going to have to stay somewhere until the shipment is unloaded, and be sure to set aside personal items that you'll need between loading and unloading, such as clothes, toiletries, and any medications. If it seems like too much time will pass before the unloading, ask about it.

Setting a moving date at the end of a month may cost extra because that's the most popular moving time. Similarly, a move in the summer might cost you more than a winter move (although summer moves might be easier and well worth the money—the day we moved into our present house, a foot of snow fell). If your move is during the winter and involves cold climates, be careful about significant time between loading and unloading; ask where your shipment will be (as in a warehouse). You don't want it to freeze.

## Move Some Items Yourself

When you're getting estimates, ask the mover to point out any items that might, in his opinion, require extra cost to handle, and consider handling those items yourself. We know of a case

118

in which the mover boxed a $100 glass-top coffee table in a specially constructed crate, at a cost of $250, without mentioning this extra cost before the move. In subsequent moves, this owner of the coffee table has been very careful to remove the glass top and transport it themselves—$250 saved.

Also, there are some items that movers won't touch. These include hazardous materials—chemicals such as bleach, aerosol cans, even nail polish—and perishable items such as plants or refrigerated foods. Ask your mover for a complete list, and clear these things out before your move or be ready to transport them yourself. In addition, it's a good idea to take responsibility for anything that's irreplaceable or has great sentimental value—you'll take the best care of such items.

# A Final Cleaning?

Remember that after you move, the new owners will be doing a final inspection before closing. You don't want them getting cold feet over a dirty house. A handy alternative to doing all the cleaning yourself is to find a good cleaning person or service; it's often cheaper than you might expect, and can save you considerable personal wear and tear on moving day.

# Unloading

When it comes to unloading, try to provide adequate space for the moving van to park. If you need to reserve some space on the street, talk to your new neighbors and ask them not to park in front of your house that day. Put up signs; you might even supplement the signs with those orange traffic cones, which you can buy at home improvement stores. Some cities will put up no-parking signs if you ask for them; consult your local police department for information.

Tell the mover about any potential access problems. If the movers have to carry loads more than 75 feet to your door, they may charge you extra.

The movers will expect you to pay with a certified check on unloading day, plus or minus a small amount, which can be handled by personal check. Before signing off on the shipment, check as carefully as you can for loss or damage. If you need extra time, take it. Don't hand over the money until you're satisfied.

# Question 20

## What Final Steps Are There?

The deal is done, and it's time to finish the process. You've gone through a lot, and no doubt you'd like to get it all off your mind for a while. But there are still some final issues that require some attention, and they are the subject of this chapter. Not all of these will apply to you, but it's a good idea to skim these topics just to be sure.

## Prepare for Possible Inquiries From the Buyer

Sometimes, buyers have questions that they want to ask after they move in — what brand and color was the house paint, does the furnace always make that noise, where is the key to the garage, and so on—and these questions are legitimate. So prepare for the fact that the buyer may be in touch with you. To avoid misunderstandings, fielding such questions can be worth your time, especially in states that have strict "lemon laws."

But at some point, the buyers are going to have to realize that it's their house now, and they're responsible for it. Providing them with reasonable help to get them settled in the house is a good thing; becoming a long-term help line for issues they should be handling themselves is not. If you feel that you're providing help on issues that should be the responsibility of any homeowner, explain that to the buyer. It's their house now, after all.

## Tie Up Loose Ends

Real estate deals are complex, and just about all of them have some loose ends that need to be tied up. For your own peace of mind, don't let loose ends dangle. Check one last time with your lawyer or escrow officer that everything's finished. More times than we'd like to count, issues turn up (sometimes demanding a check for a few hundred dollars) after a deal seems finished. If you've promised to remove some last-minute property, such as a trailer or leftover boxes, do that, too. We've seen stuff left sitting around, waiting for the previous owner to collect it, sometimes for months. That can rankle new owners who are feeling the pride of ownership, and may inflame other, smaller problems into larger ones.

> *Check one last time with your lawyer or escrow officer that everything's finished.*

## Keep Copies of All Papers

At the closing, you probably got a bale of papers and documents. Keep them. You'll probably need them when filing your taxes, because you can deduct many costs and expenses associated with the sale. You'll also need them in case you have a tax audit or some legal issue arises concerning the sale.

The HUD 1 closing statement is especially important to keep because it shows, in detail, where the money went. If you have any questions later, all you have to do is to check it (or go over it with your lawyer—those things can get very complex).

# Follow Up on Prorating Agreements

At some closings, the seller agrees to prorate some expenses whose exact costs aren't presently known, such as property taxes, with the buyer. Follow up with the buyer on those; often, they'll waive such agreements unless the amount in question is significant.

# Consider Where to Put Your Money

If you've made money from the sale, you've got to decide where to put it. These days, that can be a tough choice. Many sellers use some or all of the profits for down payment and improvements on their new house. Guard against the feeling that some sellers have, however, that the profit is "found money" that can be spent freely; you may regret that later.

Good places for the money can include buying and improving your next home, retirement planning, the stock market, even investing in additional real estate. Those who do best, we've found, have a plan for the profits they've made.

# Check to Make Sure Your Mortgage Payoff Worked

Some lending institutions are notoriously hard to work with when it comes to paying off your mortgage. Check with them that the payoff on your old mortgage actually happened, and that everything's clear. Otherwise, get the escrow officer involved immediately.

# Send Change of Address Cards

This one's pretty obvious: after you've moved, notify everyone who has to know about your change of address—credit card companies, magazines to which you subscribe, your cell phone company, online stores and service providers, friends, family, business associates, and so on. File a change of address form with the post office to get your mail forwarded.

# Make Sure the Utilities Were Switched Out of Your Name

You probably don't want to be paying for the buyer's gas, but you could be unless you've made sure the utilities were switched from your name to theirs as they should have been. Before closing, you probably arranged for all the utilities— electricity, gas/propane, telephone, cable TV, and so on—to be switched off or continued in the buyer's name. It's worthwhile to call the utility companies and check that everything actually happened as it should have, or else you've got another loose end to tie up.

> *It's worthwhile to call the utility companies and check that everything actually happened as it should have.*

# Check What Was Recorded

It's also a good idea to call the county clerk's office and make sure that your old house is no longer in your name; we've known people who received tax bills for their former property this way. If the recording wasn't done correctly; you could end up on the phone to the school district about the school taxes, the town or city about their taxes, and so on, getting the matter straightened out.

Again, if there's a problem, talk to your lawyer or escrow agent.

# Make Sure You Do the Taxes Right

Capital gains laws can change, so before you file your taxes, make sure you're doing everything right. Get a tax advisor involved if it'll help; you never know when they'll find more deductions for you.

# Keep Track of Home Improvements

If you invest some or all of the profits of the sale in improving your new home, make sure you keep track of those improvements. Keep the bills—as you know, you can add them to the cost basis of your new home, should you ever decide to sell and go through the whole process again.

# Additional Information

Cozzi, Guy. *Real Estate Home Inspection Checklist from A to Z.* Nemmar Real Estate Training, 2004.

Evans, Blanche. *Homesurfing.Net: The Insider's Guide to Buying and Selling Your Home Using the Internet.* Chicago: Dearborn Trade Publishing, 1999.

Gadow, Sandy. *The Complete Guide to Your Real Estate Closing: Answers to All Your Questions—From Opening Escrow, to Negotiating Fees, to Signing the Closing Papers.* New York: McGraw-Hill, 2002.

Irwin, Robert. *The For Sale by Owner Kit.* Chicago: Dearborn Financial Publishing, 2004.

————. *Tips and Traps When Negotiating Real Estate.* New York: McGraw-Hill, 1995.

Kozik, Donna and Tara Maras. *29 Days to a Smooth Move.* San Diego: Donna Kozik and Tara Maras, 2003. http://www.29DaysToASmoothMove.com.

Lee, Michael D. *Opening Doors: Selling to Multicultural Real Estate Customers.* Winchester, Va: Oakhill Press, 1999.

Vitt, Lois A. *10 Secrets to Successful Home Buying and Selling : Using Your Housing Psychology to Make Smarter Decisions.* Upper Saddle River, N.J.: Prentice Hall, 2005.

Webb, Martha and Sarah Parsons Zackheim. *Dress Your House for Success: 5 Fast, Easy Steps to Selling Your House, Apartment, or Condo for the Highest Possible Price!* New York: Three Rivers Press, 1997.